DR ALISTAIR TULLOCH

MEDICINE AND OTHER TOPICS

novum pro

All rights of distribution, including via film, radio, and television, photomechanical reproduction, audio storage media, electronic data storage media, and the reprinting of portions of text, are reserved.

Printed in the European Union on environmentally friendly, chlorine- and acid-free paper.

© 2023 novum publishing

ISBN 978-3-99131-561-2
Editing: Roderick Pritchard-Smith
Cover photo:
Richard Cote | Dreamstime.com
Cover design, layout & typesetting: novum publishing
Internal illustrations: Dr Alistair Tulloch

The images provided by the author have been printed in the highest possible quality.

www.novum-publishing.co.uk

Contents

Introduction 7

Chapter 1
Brief Ancestry of the Tulloch Family 9

Chapter 2
My Early Years 12

Chapter 3
The Wartime Years 1939–45 23

Chapter 4
National Service in the RAF: 1950-52 37

Chapter 5
Postgraduate Training in Worcester: 1952-54 59

Chapter 6
Starting General Practice in Coventry: 1954–63 66

Chapter 7
Change to a practice in Bicester: 1963–87 70

Chapter 8
Marriage to Christine Goffe: 1966 73

Chapter 9
GP Research Appointment: 1967–87 76

Chapter 10
Nuffield Travelling Research Fellowship
in the USA: 1972 80

Chapter 11
Care of Patients in Advanced Old Age 88

Chapter 12
The Programme of Care for Patients in Retirement 103

Chapter 13
My Political View of British Premiers since the War 107

Chapter 14
Towards retirement 116

Chapter 15
The Evolution of Western Medicine 122

Chapter 16
Looking back 138

Chapter 17
The Scots Nationalists 145

Chapter 18
Covid–19: A Viral Pandemic 148

Chapter 19
Past thoughts 150

Chapter 20
What of the Future? 155

Chapter 21
Final chapter 159

Summary of my career 161

Introduction

The idea of writing a book in the form of an autobiography crossed my mind several times in the last fifteen years only to be discarded despite the fact that I had done quite well at school. I had later written a number of medical articles and a chapter in several textbooks, but I did not feel confident about this task.

Nevertheless, it was my wife Christine who set the ball rolling again by pointing out three years ago suggesting that I ought to write a small booklet describing the variety of interesting tasks I have handled as a doctor. It was designed to entertain offspring, grandchildren and close friends. I gave some thought to this view, but I remained uncertain and as a result took no action.

However sometime later I read a book by Adam Kay, an obstetrician, called "This is Going to Hurt" which was an interesting read and a bestseller. He has much more talent than me but I am indebted to him as he changed my mind and I started to write the book. It set out to be purely an autobiography.

My career and lifestyle have been unusual to say the least and six months after graduating I was in the RAF which took me to Egypt and the Sudan. I was then a bachelor and I decided to spend two years on three hospital appointments. I never once met another GP who had done this length of postgraduate training at this stage. GPs today however would be unimpressed since they spend around four years or so in hospital and general practice while in postgraduate training. The result is that they are better trained today.

During my career I also wrote a thesis for my MD on structured records which seemed to interest only a few GPs. Subsequently, at a conference, I met the director of a computer company who said that if all GPs had introduced a structured record system the National Health Service could have saved millions. I advised the

Ministry of Health about this but they took no action. I was twice invited abroad to speak on records – at a Conference of the Italian Epidemiological Society in Rome and at the University of Los Angeles on Care of the Elderly. In the last quarter of my career I began to take a special interest in care of people in advanced old age along with a colleague, Dr David Beale, a very able clinician. We approached all the relevant Colleges but were unable to provoke any interest. Retirement came when I was 61 years of age and we bought a house in Spain which we retained for fourteen years. Thereafter we have enjoyed a variety of foreign cruises. Finally the book touches on political affairs.

I have now been retired for 31 years as compared with 37 years in practice. I still kept fit playing tennis and golf and I believe that there is still a little petrol left in the tank. Now at the age of 96 I am really quite fit despite my having aortic stenosis (a leaking heart valve). However, I am much more forgetful these days though I am still enjoying life and am still playing golf.

On the other hand the final curtain cannot be too far away. I really cannot complain as life has been very kind to me from my early days with my parents and sister. Later and most important of all with my dear wife Christine, my three children and five grandchildren. Finally I have had a circle of friends whose company also gave me great pleasure although most of them are now dead.

So the reader can see how fortunate I have been working in general practice and on retirement my wife and I visiting so many fascinating foreign countries as well as delightful cruises especially on the rivers of Europe. Now the holidays are scaled down for obvious reasons.

CHAPTER 1

Brief Ancestry of the Tulloch Family

My ancestors, whom I traced back to 1790, were based in the village of Kiltarlity, near Beauly in Invernesshire. They were poor Highland crofters who eked out a living from their modest plots of land. However, when my grandfather, Alexander Tulloch, married towards the end of the 19th century he moved to a croft called Ballachraggen in Kirkhill, a scattered village some seven miles from Inverness. There he built the family house himself and raised three children, the eldest of whom was my father, born in 1900. The tradition in the Highlands of Scotland at that time was that the first-born son took his father's name and thus my father was also called Alexander to conform to this custom as had the previous three generations.

He had one brother and one sister, both close to him in age. Father was quite the most able of the three and having passed his exams he wanted to be a doctor but the family could not afford the costs involved. Instead he started training as a bank clerk with the Commercial Bank of Scotland (CBS) in Muir-of-Ord near Inverness, in 1916.

Then, in 1918 near the end of the war he was called up for military service and spent over two years mainly with the Army of Occupation in Germany.

On his return from the army he was transferred to a branch of the bank in Castletown, near Thurso in Caithness as a medium level bank clerk. Castletown was a pleasant little village laid out, unusually for Scotland, in a modest grid pattern. Father was very happy there although the work was scarcely demanding – he started at 10 am and usually finished around 3.30 to 4pm, after which he might have some bookwork to do. However the social life in the village was very lively. Remarkably the village had two halls with plenty of scope for village social events, dances and sports such as badminton, while the Bank Manager had a private lawn tennis court – courtesy of the Commercial Bank of Scotland.

Soon after father arrived he met Bill McKenzie and they became friends. Bill ran a village butcher's business and was also an auctioneer. He lived in Castletown and was well off even if he was rather laid back about business affairs. He confided this to my father and asked him to help with his financial affairs. Dad was delighted and he soon re-organised them but refused to be paid as 'the bank wouldn't like it' which became a family joke. However Bill, who was a very generous man, insisted in rewarding father with sides of beef, lamb and chicken breast and legs etc. He also introduced father to his sister Mary and they soon began courting. She was the daughter of the now retired village butcher John McKenzie – my grandfather – who had a thriving butcher's business delivering meat to people living within a 30-mile radius of Castletown as well as supplying the village itself. Grandpa (then retired) was a real character with a great fund of amusing stories which made him excellent company for my cousin John McKenzie (son of Bill) and myself. When not at work he often wore a grey Homburg hat and a black coat which made him look more like a city gent than a village butcher.

Grannie was much more serious but nonetheless devoted to her children. They had a family of six – four sons and two daughters, the elder being my mother Mary, a woman of strong convictions, a wicked sense of humour and who was something of an entertainer. She also used a number of local dialect words, many of which I had never heard before – she said that they were "old Caithness words" which in most cases was true but she would occasionally simply fashion words of her own. The younger daughter was called Margaret – always known as Mag – also a woman of strong convictions and the brightest intellect in their home. She wanted to be a doctor and she had qualified for Edinburgh University before she was 17 but they did not take applicants aged below 18 so she deferred. She had always been good at sports and she played hockey and tennis and ultimately reached near county status. However she kept deferring the medical course and ultimately gave up on the subject. Instead she turned to gym teaching which was a surprise to everyone but she enjoyed the work and did a bit of coaching as well.

Two of her brothers, Bob and Jack emigrated to the USA and later Canada some years before the First World War. They ended up running a thriving cattle dealing business in Lacombe, Alberta, Canada. By the middle twenties they were very prosperous. Another brother, Bill (mentioned before), took over the running of the butcher's shop with a manager and he also served as an auctioneer as well as managing two farms, Castle Hill and Greenvale. Mind you, with his various forms of work he had to delegate much of the day-to-day farm work to employees. Thus he acted rather like a gentleman farmer.

The last brother had a serious accident before the Great War which left him almost permanently in pain and, as a result, he was declared unfit for military service. However he insisted that he was fit and he persuaded the Army to accept him. The Army however was to make no concessions to his disability except that that he was not to be a fighting soldier. As a result he was obliged to do long hours on the parade ground 'square bashing'. In addition, he was not exempt from having to carry around heavy equipment and keeping fit just like a fighting soldier. As a result he suffered much more pain and he was a sick man on discharge from the service. As a result, tragically, he was to die in 1922. He had always been known as the 'iron man' of the McKenzie family.

My mother, Mary Mackenzie and her parents had been crofters, but one of my grandfather's brothers drank the family out of the croft. However, her father, John McKenzie, immediately set up as a butcher, serving Castletown and about 30 miles around. He quite steadily built up the business across the years and by the time I was going there in the late twenties he had retired. Of all my grandparents he was the one I liked most although my grannie was very kind to my cousin John McKenzie and me as well. We were up to all sorts of mischief but she saved us from punishment time and again.

CHAPTER 2

My Early Years

In due course Father married Mary McKenzie and within a year I was born on May 31st, 1926, in Manu House, a big house built by a retired sea captain years before – the rather odd name came from somewhere in China as he had worked mainly in the Orient. The house was divided into flats, one of which was all my parents could afford in the twenties. The great event of this era was the General Strike, which had created an upheaval some weeks earlier in 1926. There was also the matter of what name I was to be given since Mother had found Alexander 'rather a mouthful' but she did not want to offend the Tullochs. So she settled for Alistair – the Gaelic for Alexander and only a little less of a mouthful.

Perth 1927

A year later in 1927 Father was transferred to the Perth branch of the Bank and promoted from bank clerk to 'accountant' which was a bank ranking in those days rather than the financial affairs professional of today.

Stow, Midlothian 1928

After a year there we moved to Stow, a lovely village on the river Gala about 26 miles from Edinburgh. There Dad was to be a bank manager and he was told he was the youngest in the CBS, but to begin with he was under the surveillance of the manager from a bigger branch in nearby Galashiels – it was however a largely nominal supervision. Father incidentally was aged 27 at this point and we came to live in a bigger house than either of my parents had experienced before, part of which was the bank office. They thought they had landed in clover, especially as they had a large garden and father was a keen gardener. We were to spend twelve happy years there and looking back I feel that no children could have been more fortunate than my sister and I to live in such an attractive area with devoted parents and a lively social life. I joined the village gang of boys and we soon got up to the usual forms of mischief. We were also very interested in football, rugby and tennis which I started playing at the age of nine.

Primary School Stow, Midlothian 1933

I recall clearly starting school in Stow and I particularly remember the first day at school for two reasons. There was a world map on the wall, almost half of which was coloured in red to identify parts of the British Empire and of course at the age five I had no idea what an empire was. After school I also tripped on the kerb later that first day and gashed my knee which required stitches not given in most cases at that time. I can recall this episode quite clearly today nearly ninety years afterwards because of the acute pain when the needle went through the skin on each side of the cut. Nonetheless I really enjoyed my time at Stow school and I nearly always came first in the class, which led me to believe I was more able than was the case. Of course most of my fellow pupils came mainly from a more modest background than me and were rarely strong performers, probably as they did not have parents encouraging them to 'stick in' as mine did. Stow was a commuter village for those who worked in Edinburgh and there were a good few more affluent families there than ours. Their children were usually privately educated in Edinburgh and so we saw them much less often than the locals. Incidentally the private school system in Scotland differs from the English public school system since most of the private pupils are non-resident and based mainly in the bigger cities or nearby. However there are also some four or five residential private schools in various parts of the country based on the English school system, which catered for wealthy families, the aristocracy and even the odd member of the Royal Family. Incidentally I knew very little about the English educational system before I came down to England in 1950 to do my National Service in the RAF. I was simply bewildered by the cost especially of the most expensive 'public schools' like Eton and Harrow – I put the term in inverted commas as nothing on earth seemed to me to be less public than a public school.

Stow was in the middle of a fertile area of Scotland and my impression was that the farmers in the district were more prosperous than in many other parts of Scotland. However my father claimed that the Black Isle (near Inverness) provided the best farming soil in Scotland, a view contested by several other Scots friends. Dad was a proud Highlander and not always highly objective on matters of this sort but he was the most encouraging of fathers.

I was active in the local group of boys and we were up to every mischief under the sun but sometimes things went too far. On one occasion I was the perpetrator and to this day I feel a sense of guilt when the subject comes up. Although I was a small boy I suffered very little from bullying at school but one boy in the class used to 'ping' my ears, which was very humiliating in company. I asked him to stop but he paid no attention and since he was much bigger than me there was little I could do about it. So I decided to give him a good soaking in the hope that he would end the 'pinging'. This was to be achieved by dropping a flat stone near him as he emerged from under a bridge on which I was seated. He had been fishing for minnows with four of our friends. Now as the stone left my hand, to my horror he moved to the right towards the falling stone which clipped him on the side of the head opening a cut which bled freely and friends on the spot came to his assistance. To my shame I rushed home hoping that I would avoid retribution but my Mother soon recognised that something was amiss.

So I had to explain what had happened and by this time the boy had turned up at our house seeking help. Mother dressed his wound and took him to the doctor who put in a couple of stitches. On her return she gave me 'two of the best' on each hand adding 'you deserved more'. Next day came the second half of the punishment – the headmaster hauled me out in front of the school and criticised me for cowardly behaviour in dropping the stone and (even worse) departing the scene after the accident. He then added: 'You might easily have seriously injured or even killed Archie', which was of course quite true and I felt terribly guilty. I even considered running away as I did not seem to have a friend in the world at this point. So I had nobody to run to for support. Mind you, in another three days I was back in favour as one of the boys again.

We were a lively class, given sometimes to whispering or even occasionally chattering in lessons, which did not go down at all well with the teachers and occasionally they resorted to punishment with a thick leather belt with thongs, known to the pupils as "the belt" or "the tawse" or "the tug", administered to the hands. Of course nobody wanted this punishment but anyone who had it became a class hero and thus it did have the desired result. In due course teachers recognised this and resorted instead to expelling the offender from class which was much more effective. The reason for this was that one felt very lonely outside the class door and there was always the fear that the headmaster would come along and ask why the expulsion had been ordered. This often led to the importance of not making the teacher's job more difficult but if he felt that the offence was more serious the belt was used as punishment administered sometimes by the headmaster himself in his room.

My time in Stow, from 1928 to 1940, was, in retrospect, a real pleasure to me and I made a series of friends with whom I played a variety of sports – football and a rather tame form of rugby in the winter, and in the summer a crude form of cricket as well as fishing for minnows in the Gala River, which also deepened in one place enabling us to use it for swimming. We even started to play tennis in 1935 and I was to play the game for the next 70 years. As I now look back down the years, my impression is that the summers in the thirties were almost eternally warm and sunny enabling us to enjoy these pleasures: Or is it simply distance lending enchantment to the view?

The arrival of my sister Margaret 1935

Nineteen thirty-five saw the arrival of my sister Margaret after a difficult pregnancy for Mother who had severe and persistent sickness known to the medical profession as hyperemesis gravidarum – doctors have a weakness for imposing names. Then she went from bad to worse and the doctors warned my father that she may die unless she was admitted to a private ward in hospital. There the doctors tried everything and they did slow the rate of decline. However Mother was becoming concerned about the steadily mounting costs of private inpatient hospital care, which Father could ill afford. As a result she suddenly announced that she was going home, to the dismay of the doctors including her GP, in whom she normally had great faith. They told her that if she did go home she was much more likely to die. Her response was simply to say: 'If I am going to die I would prefer to die at home rather than in hospital'. Poor Father by this time was broken hearted since there was no sign of improvement and he felt sure she was going to die. However she proved both him and the doctors wrong as she turned the corner and began to improve slowly some three to four days after her return. Thereafter the recovery continued slowly but steadily and she had a normal delivery some six months later, a baby girl weighing eight and half pounds. I fear it must be said that I viewed her arrival with mixed feelings since I alone had been the centre of attention for the previous nine years and this state of affairs was now coming to an end. She was a large noisy baby who howled blue murder if she did not get her way and this did not help to endear her to me at first. Indeed, we fought tooth and nail for several years, after which she became much more amenable and grew into a charming young woman. We remained close friends for the rest of our lives. In the end she was to die sadly a very unpleasant death as a result of a neuro-degenerative disorder, rather similar to motor neurone disease.

At this time another pleasure was going to 'the pictures' as the cinema was then called in Scotland and even today seventy years later I can recall the most popular films of this period clearly. Humour came from American films starring Stan Laurel and Oliver Hardy, with Stan nearly always looking gormless while Oliver was pompous and self-righteous but nearly always wrong in the end. Then there was Mickey Rooney in the Andy Hardy series with Judy Garland as his girlfriend before she became primarily a songbird. However the most memorable film of that era was "Gone with the Wind" starring Clark Gable and Vivian Leigh, which reached Britain in 1939.

Summer Holidays in Caithness 1928–40

Each summer we went as a family to the home of my mother's parents in Castletown, Caithness, although we seemed to spend most of our time at Manu House where I was born. This was now a family home again since my Uncle Bill had bought it. He was always busy and had a well-developed sense of humour. His son John was my main sparring partner among the local lads and he had a sister called Lilian. There was almost no foreign travel for ordinary families at this time therefore some of my mother's contemporaries from her schooldays brought their families up to Caithness each year for their holidays. So John and I had plenty of company each summer playing the same games, lounging on the beach and fishing from a small boat called 'The Girl Pat' belonging to an experienced sailor called Ittle who was full of tales of life at sea – to our great delight.

One evening John and I went out fishing alone and we began to find we were further offshore than we had planned. So we decided to row back and we found it hard work. Well, at that point fins began to appear around the boat which, we thought to our dismay, were from sharks. Of course we did not know then that sharks rarely appear in the Pentland Firth, especially inshore. So we were extremely frightened and we decided to row back very slowly so as not to annoy the 'sharks'. They were however in no way aggressive and after a relatively short period, to our great relief, they departed. Next day we reported our experience to Ittle who said, with a smile they were almost certainly not sharks but were far more likely to be friendly dolphins!

What made this holiday crowd so congenial was that they were parents who had been to school with my mother – mainly female but there were a few males. They made it clear that we had to observe the rules and one of these was 'no smoking'. Otherwise we had carte blanche and for most of the time we did observe the rules but not all the time. These summer holidays were always a great source of pleasure to me each year and they cost my parents very little. It is a quite different story today.

I look back on these Caithness holidays, especially in the thirties, with great pleasure although sometimes John and I got ourselves into hot water. John always had much more pocket money than me which enabled us to buy cigarettes – Wild Woodbines to be precise. When we smoked them there was a wonderful feeling of defying authority in doing something which had been forbidden by our parents. However when we were caught the pleasure gave way to dismay at the thought of punishment. On one occasion, for example, while we were smoking, one of us carelessly threw away a lighted match which set several raspberry bushes alight (it had been a very hot summer) and we were caught in the act. A long lecture followed on the evils of smoking and the threat of physical punishment if we smoked again. On another occasion later, I well remember that Cousin John and I were having a few days sleeping in a tent on the links beside the beach in Castletown. We had not smoked for some weeks although we did have a few Wild Woodbines left. The question arose whether we could allow ourselves just one 'fag'. In the end we decided that one each was acceptable, and as you might imagine this soon became five or six each and the interior of the tent became just like a bar room in those days. We were utterly relaxed and at peace with the world when to our horror the flap of the tent was cast back and a familiar face appeared – it was my Dad and he played things very cool. He remarked that: 'Your Mother required me to drop in and ask you whether there was anything you needed.' I replied, 'No, not really' and with that he departed saying, 'See you in the morning.' We, of course, were very anxious as to whether he had noticed that we had been smoking. This was utterly ridiculous in retrospect as Dad could hardly miss the pungent smell of smoke which also permeated the inside of the tent. Nonetheless we managed to persuade ourselves that he just hadn't noticed the smoke in the tent.

Next morning we felt that it might be wise for us to stay away from the house until lunch and when we did arrive no mention was made of smoking. However Dad raised the subject after lunch and he added that he was very disappointed that I had not kept my promise to give up smoking. As a result of this misbehaviour I was unable to go to a picnic to which I was looking forward very much. I was quite convinced I would never smoke again.

A period without smoking then followed after which the temptation was too much and John and I shared a fag in the butcher's van when the van man had finished his work. However unfortunately he returned to retrieve something from the vehicle and caught us in the act.

The van driver was a heavy smoker himself but he was emphatic that we should never smoke and to drive home his point he inhaled from his cigarette and blew the smoke through his white handkerchief leaving a dark brown stain on it. That he said in a sepulchral tone was what is left on your lungs each time you smoke and inhale. I was most impressed by this and as a result I never developed the smoking habit again. John went on smoking and developed emphysema at the end of his life but he did live into his middle eighties. Geordie, the van man, also carried on smoking and he was to die from lung cancer when he was in his seventies.

Cousin John and I looked forward with keen anticipation to our annual summer holidays each year. This phase of life is one that most children enjoy and we were no exception. Football was the main sport but we also played rugby, tennis and occasionally badminton. Summer saw us bathing in the River Gala and fishing for minnows. On the other hand in the Autumn and Winter we would swim in the indoor pool in Galashiels some seven miles away.

The Thirties

The cinema came into my life in the late thirties first with Mickey Rooney playing Andy Hardy and Judy Garland as his girlfriend. Judy also starred in the 'The Wizard of Oz' at this time which sent us all singing 'Somewhere Over the Rainbow'. Then, shortly before war broke out, there was 'Gone with the Wind a smash hit with Clark Gable, Vivian Leigh and Leslie Howard. At this stage of my life I was, like most schoolboys, unaware of the gathering storm in Nazi Germany, although I had heard of Hitler who was being lampooned in the "Just William" series of books by Richmal Compton– another great favourite of mine at the time. William was forever in mischief and he served as a model for Cousin John and I. Then, in 1939 came the first National Black-out dummy run and only then did I realise the seriousness of the situation. In 1938 I passed the Qualifying Examination (equivalent of the 11 Plus in England) and started my secondary education at Dalkeith High School, near Edinburgh, which involved a 36-mile round journey by rail each day. I was somewhat surprised to find that I was no longer first in the class in any subject, my best subjects being History, French and English. The star pupil in my year was called Tony and he was the son of a railway signalman. He was remarkable as he never failed to get 100% in mathematics at school. I once beat him in a history exam and I could not wait to get home to tell my parents about this success. He was also a mid-to long-distance runner of national standard and who became a professor of mathematics.

At Dalkeith we were introduced to organised sport for the first time and I soon enjoyed it very much. To this day I can remember the first rugby match I played in as scrum half for the third school team at the age of thirteen years. I would like to report that it was a glorious victory but alas it was a mismatch and we were thrashed!

About this time my parents, who were both ardent Conservatives, took me to a political fete in Boland near Stow in the Scots border country. Addressing the faithful was a prominent Conservative MP called Captain A H Maule Ramsay, a member of the local aristocracy. He launched into a blistering attack on the Jews who he claimed were the source of most of the evils of the world. At the end of his speech he was red faced with the sustained ranting. Ramsay belonged to a vein of Conservative aristocracy in Scotland and England some of whom were pro-Hitler and in contact with the Nazis. Soon after the Second World War began Ramsey was jailed as a threat to the conduct of the war and he was only released in 1944. It was reported later that if Hitler had invaded Britain in 1940 Maule Ramsay was to have been made the Gauleiter (Nazi Leader) for Scotland, a fact which we learned much later.

In the period just before the war began there was a great scare about Nazi spies coming ashore from German submarines or being dropped from planes at night. In fact there were very few of these spies and those there were appeared to have been poorly trained and were often given away by their guttural accents. However the public were urged to report anyone behaving suspiciously. Thus one evening when we were returning from school a man came into our train compartment who looked just like our idea of a spy as projected in the cinema. He wore a black hat and coat and had darkly tinted glasses. In addition he had a bulky object in his right trouser pocket which we imagined was a gun. So we reported him to the guard on the train who said he would be arrested in Galashiels, the station after Stow, our destination.

We never heard any news subsequently that a spy had been arrested and so I assume he was an innocent man but the story shows how we were caught up in the spy scare of the pre-war period. We always think that everything the Germans do is likely to be very carefully organised but their spy programme at the beginning of the war was exactly the reverse.

Alistair and his parents, Mary and Alexander Tulloch on his wedding day 26 November 1966

CHAPTER 3

The Wartime Years 1939–45

We were all aware at this point that war was imminent and so it was no surprise on September 3rd, 1939 when Prime Minister Neville Chamberlain declared war on Germany as a result of the German refusal to guarantee Belgian and Polish neutrality. My Father was a Regional Officer in the ARP (Air Raid Precautions) and he had to visit several parts of his region that day to ensure that everything was in place. On his return he forecast that the German bombers would be over within a few hours but in fact it proved the beginning of six months of 'phoney war' as the Nazis prepared for their Blitzkrieg (lightening war) in Belgium, Holland and France, utterly undetected by the French and British intelligence systems. Some bombs did in fact fall on a tiny village – a minor railway junction seven miles from Stow, where we lived – called Fountainhall. Almost no damage was done and clearly they had bombed the wrong target. Next morning a boy from Fountainhall distributed bits of shrapnel to his fellow pupils on the train en route to school. This was to be the nearest I ever came to a bomb during the war.

The German Blitzkrieg in Belgium and Northern France in Spring 1940 was, by contrast, a great success for them, due to excellent planning and execution by the Wehrmacht (German Army) helped by poor British intelligence and indifferent forward planning on the Allied side. The German Army swept rapidly across Belgium, Holland and Northern France helped by close co-operation with the Luftwaffe (German Air Force) right up to ten miles from Dunkirk. Herr Hitler, to the astonishment of everyone on both sides and to the dismay of many of his generals, ordered his troops to halt. It was thought at first that he feared that the German soldiers would be exhausted and decided to give them a rest. However the reality nowadays is thought to be quite different. Hitler greatly admired the British Empire and he knew that there were Nazi sympathisers in this country, especially among the aristocracy. As a result he hoped to strike an agreement with the British which would maintain the Empire intact – within the Third Reich of course. However Churchill was vigorously opposed to doing a deal with Hitler, who had ordered Hermann Goering leader of the Luftwaffe to eradicate the remnants of the British Army following the Dunkirk withdrawal.

Although the British Army suffered a dreadful mauling on the beach at Dunkirk in the circumstances they showed remarkable resilience. Thus when a fleet of ships of all types, from small sailing vessels to Royal Navy destroyers, arrived they proved remarkably successful in collecting the remaining soldiers and ferrying them back to the UK. It was hailed at the time as something of a miracle. Well we did evacuate many more troops than we expected or should have been allowed by the Germans at Dunkirk although the troops left all their armour (tanks, guns etc) behind. This was the period of the war when the national morale was at its lowest ebb. At this point the French had surrendered while the British Army, having lost so much of its armaments was for the time being highly vulnerable. Furthermore, Hitler had ordered an invasion of Britain under the name of Operation Sealion and he began to assemble a fleet of boats near to Calais for this purpose. However when he presented his plans to Goering, Admiral Raeder and his most senior generals, they were almost wholly opposed to Hitler's plans. The reason for this was that they could not guarantee the safety of troops crossing even the 29 miles from Calais to Dover with the much bigger and more powerful Royal Navy on hand. Hitler was forced to take their advice and postpone the invasion which saved our bacon in 1940.

Life in Inverurie, Aberdeenshire 1940–50

In 1940 Father was transferred to Inverurie in Aberdeenshire, at this point to manage the local branch of the Commercial Bank of Scotland and when he arrived he found some of the troops retrieved from the Dunkirk beaches had been transferred to the town. For the first night some were obliged to sleep in the street. However, thereafter local families took them into their homes and the next day they were moved into the town hall.

The brigadier in charge happened to choose Dad's bank to handle the soldiers' finances and he rang up one day seeking to withdraw quite a large sum of money, which had to be carefully organised. When they had made arrangements Dad added jocularly 'and the usual armed guard I suppose?' Imagine his surprise when the next morning the Brigadier appeared with an armed guard of eight soldiers who lined up four on each side of the bank entrance while the cash was carried out to an Army vehicle. As a result, a rumour swept the town that the new Bank Manager was a German spy and had been arrested! Dad dined out on that story for years afterwards.

Inverurie was a quite prosperous Aberdeenshire market town although most of the labourers and engineers in town were employed in the Railway Repair Depot. The war-time years saw us go from the dire pessimism of the early forties when the Nazis seemed certain to win the war after their astonishing victory in the 'Blitzkrieg' which led to the beaches of Dunkirk. This was a serious defeat with many of our troops killed or captured but the remarkable withdrawal of the residue of the British Army from Dunkirk gave us the first modest hint of optimism. However, much of the armour (guns, tanks etc) of the British Army had to be left in France and without it any hopes of victory seemed remote. So when the French sought help from the British Army after the Dunkirk withdrawal, the British generals were none too keen. Churchill, as a gesture, asked Air Chief Marshall Sir Hugh Dowding, the Head of Fighter Command, to send six fighter squadrons of the RAF to France. Dowding, always revered by his men, refused, as he anticipated that the Battle of Britain was about to start and he felt that we needed to retain all the planes in our possession for this coming struggle. How right he was.

This was the rock bottom period of the war with the British public almost certain that we were to be invaded and defeated. It was hard to believe otherwise, but the German service chiefs were very apprehensive about what the Royal Navy might be able to do to any invasion force. Consequently they persuaded Hitler to postpone the invasion which, as pointed out earlier, saved our bacon. However most historians believe that it also saved the German Navy for lack of U Boats at that point. Later in the War it was a different story as the German Navy in 1943 had far more submarines, called U-boats, which were threatening to win the Battle of the Atlantic. Our losses were heavy but we held them, especially when the United States entered the War and the pendulum swung our way.

Battle of Britain June – September 1940

Then came the Battle of Britain, the only battle then and now fought solely in the air, and few of us realised at the time how crucial it was to be to our survival. It was feared that the Luftwaffe would prove too strong, but we had great faith in the RAF and particularly in the Spitfires, although the Hurricanes were to shoot down twice as many German planes as the Spitfires during the few months of the battle. The Hurricane was the oldest plane (designed in the late twenties) of the three fighter planes and thus was slower than the other two. However it had a tighter turn and was more strongly built than either of the others, which meant that it was harder to shoot down. In addition British pilots were more likely to survive a crash or crash landing if flying the Hurricane or Spitfire was involved. RAF staff also learned a good deal about the Me109 when they were shot down.

The other two planes were designed on the same premise of a light body and a powerful engine to achieve maximum speed. The main German fighter plane was the Messerschmitt 109 (or Bf 109 – the official German name) which was an excellent fighting machine. It was better armoured with six or eight cannons which were more destructive than the Spitfire's eight machine guns. The Me 109 also had petrol injection engines rather than the carburettors fitted to the British machines in the early stages of the war. Thus, experienced German pilots learned to force British planes into a steep dive which often led the engine to cut out and as a result for some seconds they became sitting ducks as a result. The Spitfire was, however, slightly slower but it had a tighter turn than the Me 109 which proved vital in many dog fights. The Me 109's space for ammunition was also more limited than that of the Spitfire which often proved important in a dogfight. In addition, our pilots were better trained than their German opposite numbers since the Luftwaffe had only been allowed to train their pilots since 1935 under the Geneva Convention of 1918. On the other hand, some German pilots who had fought in the Spanish Civil War had gained valuable experience in this field. The main problem for the Luftwaffe was that they were fighting an away fixture and when shot down Germen pilots were killed or captured and were thus out of the war, whereas British pilots could return to the fray if they had survived. The German pilots also had to keep a close eye on the amount of petrol in their tanks and sometimes they had to break off a dogfight they might be dominating to ensure that they did not run out of petrol on the way back.

The Luftwaffe pilots were also understandably apprehensive about landing in the Channel, which, in the early days, meant almost certain death. However, the Germans later organised a rescue service for those who survived after a crash. In addition Air Chief Marshall Dowding and his deputy Air Marshall Keith Park (a New Zealander) handled the RAF much better than Goering did during the battle, as the latter badly underestimated the important role of radar and the Royal Observer Corps, who provided early warnings of incoming Luftwaffe planes. Goering also underestimated the number of British fighter planes available for battle as well as under construction. We also turned our planes out faster than the Germans, especially later in the battle.

Since the war there has been endless debate as to which side had the better planes but the matter was not that simple. The RAF pilots knew they had to win the battle which they fought with great skill and bravery, as did their opponents. This led to a mutual respect between the two air forces which is reflected in a famous story. Hermann Goering, head of the Luftwaffe, asked one of his most successful air aces, Adolf Galland, what was needed to defeat the RAF. Galland replied bravely: 'Six squadrons of Spitfires, Sir', which infuriated Goering. However, Galland knew that he was taking on an excellent plane in the Spitfire but he also knew that he had a match in the Me 109.

Also to my delight I found that one of the top RAF aces, James "Ginger" Lacey was a second cousin of mine. He also became a national figure when he shot down the plane that had bombed Buckingham Palace. The King then asked the RAF if he and his family could meet the pilot responsible, which was arranged at short notice and the meeting was shown in our local cinema in Inverurie. The manager of the cinema was a client of my father in the Commercial Bank of Scotland and he invited our family to a private showing of the meeting, which we ran through seven or eight times. So Lacey became a national hero. By the end of the battle he had shot down 18 German planes plus a few 'probables' and was the second highest scoring English ace in the Battle of Britain.

The link to a war time hero was a matter of pride for a 13-year-old boy and of course I made the most of it, although I never met Lacey during the war or indeed ten years later when I joined the RAF to do my National Service as a Medical Officer. He had been a pharmacy student but left to join the RAF around the start of the war. His hobby had been target shooting in a club which made him also an accurate shot in the air, and he liked to get as close as possible to the enemy to achieve greater accuracy.

Curiously, the RAF seemed to feel that his technique was too valuable for him to stay on active operations for most of the rest of the war and I was told that he spent much of the time teaching less experienced fighter pilots. However I think I am right in saying that he shot down a further ten planes during the rest of the war.

The Battle of Britain ended in late September with the sides very evenly balanced and with Goering over-confident that the Luftwaffe was going to win. His strategy early in the Battle had been to bomb a convoy in the Channel, which attracted fighter planes (mainly Hurricanes) from south coast aerodromes. This enabled the Luftwaffe to send in bombers which did considerable damage to cities like Portsmouth, Southampton and Plymouth.

Then the Germans switched their attacks onto south coast airfields used by Hurricanes mainly and their practice was to destroy the runways to prevent fighters taking off safely. Then they would send in fighter bombers such as the Messerschmitt 110 which had been very successful in support of the Wehrmacht during the Blitzkrieg at the start of the war. However during the Battle of Britain the Hurricanes found them easy to shoot down and the German losses were very heavy as a result. In addition, the British quickly learned how to repair the runways and the Germans had to change their strategy again.

Hitler had started the struggle ordering the Luftwaffe to avoid bombing civilians but when Churchill ordered the bombing of Berlin he responded with heavy raids on London, Birmingham, Liverpool and Glasgow. This resulted in the Battle of Britain ending in some four months but the losses were grievous on both sides. However, to quote Wellington 'it was a damn close-run thing' and even the Commander-in Chief of Fighter Command, Air Chief Marshall Sir Hugh Dowding, agreed after the battle was over. Yet he had outmanoeuvred the much more experienced Hermann Goering who had been an air ace in the First World War in the Richthofen squadron. Historians today suggest that it was very close to a draw because the Me 109 shot down more Hurricanes and Spitfires than they lost themselves. Nonetheless when Hitler ordered the Luftwaffe to bomb London instead of the southern airfields it proved a serious error. Also, Goering lost the tactical battle with Dowding and our fighters found it easy to shoot down other German planes like the Me 110. Thus in the end we had shot down more German planes than we lost ourselves. More important still, Hitler had to postpone Operation Sea Lion – the planned invasion of England.

Air Training Corp & Royal Observer Corps

I remember this period in my life remarkably clearly since in 1943 I was a 17-year old Air Training Corps cadet in the RAF learning about basic navigation, the way the service was organised and the basics of flying.

While in the ATC I was among the team winners of an Aircraft Recognition Competition and the Prize was to be attached to the local Royal Observer Corps unit near my home in Aberdeenshire. These units were scattered all over the country and proved very valuable in giving an early warning, alongside radar, to the RAF of enemy aircraft approaching during the war. It was the nearest thing to active service I provided at this time. The ROC were given full details of the latest British, US and enemy planes well before they were released to the public which made me feel very privileged and more important than I was.

I clearly remember the day that we received details of the 'Schwalbe' (German for 'swallow'), later to become the Messerschmitt 262, the only jet plane on either side to go into squadron service during the war. The Air Ministry were very apprehensive about the plane, which was much faster than any UK or US plane at the time. However it had been rushed into service near the end of the war without proper trials and, as a result, it posed few problems to RAF pilots.

Progress in the war at last

Thereafter the war moved on and the pendulum began to swing in our direction with victory ultimately in the Western Desert of North Africa as well as Italy where the Germans fought a skilful defensive battle with heavy losses on both sides. However from 1940 to 1944 most of the battles were fought abroad and thus we – the British public – felt less directly involved as had been the case during the Battle of Britain. The exception was Bomber Command's offensive at first against industrial and later domestic targets. The resultant loss of RAF and civilian German lives was dreadful and unproductive. In the end the British public began to feel sympathy with both parties.

For a time the German U-Boat campaign, especially in the Atlantic, was most successful and the heavy losses of our shipping, with the important supplies they carried, made it look at one point as if we might lose the war. However we gradually gained the upper hand by way of bombing from the RAF while the Navy attacked with depth charges and we bombed the German U-boat repair bases on the French west coast.

Of course our troops were also heavily involved in fighting in the Far East against the Japanese who drove our troops back all the way to the Indian border. At this point General Bill Slim was appointed Commander of the Far East Army, the man who was in my view the best British general both strategically and tactically during the Second World War. He kept very close to his troops who always admired him enormously and was never referred to as anything but Bill Slim by junior officers or Uncle Bill by other ranks. Moreover his troops drove the Japs back despite the fighting being often in a jungle setting with which the enemy was more familiar. Yet he was often successful and always the most modest of men. When the Americans entered the war in 1941 we had started to gain the upper hand and we became more optimistic about the outcome.

Then the Russians, who had suffered a series of heavy defeats with grievous loss of life and with the Wehrmacht but they held back the Germans at the very gates of Moscow. The Germans however were defeated by a terrible winter and the rising spirits of the Russian soldiers who had suffered grievous losses previously. At this point Stalin made an important move. He had always been paranoid towards political and military figures reaching high positions, even if they had done him no harm. He feared they would overthrow him, and as a result he had them imprisoned and this had led to some of his best generals being under arrest when badly needed. As a result he decided to release some of the latter and it proved a very successful move. Perhaps the best of this group was General Rokossovsky, who proved to be the best Russian field general of the war.

The pivotal battle of this war was the Battle of Stalingrad in 1942.The losses on each side were grievous and the two armies fought each other to a standstill between August 1942 and January 1943. In the end the Russians won, and large numbers of German soldiers were taken prisoner. The tide began to turn in favour of Russia. Russian general, Marshall Zhukov was the first to arrive in Berlin with his troops in1945.

Finally, the opening of the Second Front in June1944 seemed to bring war back to our doorstep. The British and American armies made a good start on D Day but the Germans, also fought a remarkable rear guard action in Normandy and later, near Caen in particular. Thereafter they broke the German defences and set out for the Rhineland en route to Germany itself.

At the same time on the Eastern front the Russians had gained the upper hand and they had the Nazis in retreat. Victory was in sight and it came in September 1945 when the Russians entered Berlin and the Second World War was soon over. The British and American armies had hoped to get there first but it was not to be. This was due to a difference of planning by Montgomery and Eisenhower. Monty favoured a relatively narrow force which would cross the Rhine and attack the German flank from the north much as the Germans had done in reverse in 1940. It was probably the better of the two plans providing the enemy intelligence had failed. Alas it had been successful and the Germans were waiting for us fully prepared. The initial part of this battle was at Arnhem at which we were badly defeated. Meantime General Eisenhower's much broader attack was proceeding steadily and the American army were the first to enter Germany on the Western Front. Alas the Russians had arrived there first but there was a certain justice in this outcome as they had endured much heavier losses than the Western armies. The battle was over and soon after the Germans surrendered. It was the end of a terrible conflict with enormous loss of life and human suffering. The relief was expressed by the manner in which we celebrated VE Day with crowds out in every village, town and city in the land. Now and then however we would see a small minority who were wistful, sad or in tears from time to time. This was the price they had to bear for the celebration of those who had not lost a relative or close friend in the war.

Mind you, living as my family did in Aberdeenshire throughout the Second World War we barely knew their appalling loss of life. The nearest bombs to us fell on Fountainhall, seven miles from Stow and Aberdeen, fifteen miles from Inverurie the town in which we lived during most of the war. Thus we suffered much less than the English in London and the south-east although Clydebank in Glasgow did suffer a number of very heavy raids on the shipyards.

The School and University years: 1938–1950

At this stage of the war I was making my way through secondary education at the Inverurie Academy which had a legendary reputation due to the quality of the teachers and particularly the headmaster – the formidable Dr Lawson. When he asked any teacher to give additional coaching to a promising student the teacher would respond instantly although no additional payment was involved. The staff would respond in this way for the greater glory of the school. As a result a boy from Inverurie Academy had won the Bursary Prize for the best student of his year at Aberdeen University in Medicine two years earlier, only for a classmate of mine to repeat this feat in 1944. Now this was a remarkable achievement when you think that these prize winners were in competition with all the secondary schools in the North East of Scotland plus a number of boys (usually with Scottish parents) from the rest of Scotland and England.

My intention had been to take a degree in French and German after which I intended to go into the Civil Service. Now when I told Dad about this he was clearly disappointed and it transpired that he had hoped I would choose the career from which he had been barred for lack of funds – medicine. However, I thought medicine was not for me as I felt I might well pass out at the sight of blood.

Then some weeks later Dr Lawson had a meeting with my class which gradually became concerned with a discussion of our career intentions at that point and from time to time he would take one of the pupils aside for a private discussion. Since we were taken in alphabetical order my turn came late in the day and our session was a brief one in which I told him my intentions with which he expressed surprise. Then after a short interval he added: "I think you would have made a good doctor". This surprised me as my favourite subject remained History but I had told him I did not want to teach. I began to think that my father had been in touch with him but Dad strenuously denied this. So I felt that my mind was made up and there was no changing it.

Then some two weeks later I went to the library across the Square from our house to return a book, only to find a queue of five or six people ahead of me. As I waited I picked up a book on careers to pass the time and just by chance it fell open at Medicine. As I read the ten or twelve pages on this subject, I came to realise that I had never made a serious attempt to review the matter properly or consider medicine as a career choice. Suddenly it seemed more interesting and thus more appealing in this respect. However I had not yet changed my mind although strangely my fear of the sight of blood had gone. So I went to see Dr Lawson who seemed to be pleased that I was considering medicine as a career on his advice, but he felt that if there was any doubt in my mind I should consider all aspects of the subject before taking a final decision. He also pointed out that I would have to cover Higher Science in 18 months alongside two other subjects while the rest of the class took three years. The Headmaster also advised me to seek the advice of the Science master who was not an admirer of mine as I had dropped his subject and taken German instead. He told me bluntly that I was taking on a massive challenge since I would have to cover the entire field of science supplemented by experimental work and he had no time to give me private tuition. He kept stressing that he did not think the task was beyond me but the tone of his remarks suggested otherwise. It was an honest opinion and I began to have second thoughts. Some days later, by which time I had more or less given up on medicine, a girl, who was one of the two best science students in my class, approached me and asked about my problem. When I had explained it to her she replied: 'Of course you can do it, but you will have to work *very* hard. As regards the experimental work, all students get stuck now and then but I will help if required. She also forecast that when Mr B**** (the teacher) found out that I was buckling down he also would offer to help (a forecast which was later realised). I knew then that, provided I passed the Higher Grade Science examination, it was Medicine for me. Then for the next two years I rose at 6.30am each morning and worked for two hours each day before I went to school, plus Sundays. I also had to do my routine homework in the evenings. So as the examination approached I was feeling tired and I decided to end studies and rest for the last three days which recharged the batteries. I took the exam and passed quite comfortably.

The date was now September 1944 and the end of the war was in sight although it was to last the best part of another year. At this point I would have been called up to one of the Services but I was exempt because of my medical studies, although the service was deferred rather than cancelled. So I resigned from both the Air Training Corps and the Royal Observer Corps and went up to Aberdeen University to study medicine. The late forties are always described these days as 'the grey years after the war' but looking back now that is not the way I recall them. Mind you our food was still rationed and there was a great deal of austerity for the next ten to twelve years. However students are well known for kicking up their heels and we were no exception. The study of medicine is very hard work as there is so much ground to be covered and this calls for a systematised approach to study. I soon found that I was no more than a face in the crowd academically especially as the most talented student in our year was exceptionally bright and was to become a Professor of Medicine in one of the top London Medical Schools in his early thirties. The big hurdle in the early years was Anatomy – a massive grind in those days – and once over that hurdle the rest was more straightforward until Finals which lasted the best part of a fortnight. This covered written papers, orals and side room work which involved investigations. The examiners were aware of the strain on students and most tried to relax them so that they would perform to their optimum standards. However there was one exception, an English professor of obstetrics who had been knighted for looking after the Royal Family and was impatient with underperforming students. The joke was that he had roasted medical students for breakfast and – to my dismay – I found that I had drawn him for the Finals Viva Examination (Orals in Scotland). In the event he was exceedingly courteous to me, partly, I believe, because my predecessor had performed poorly and aroused his anger. He even spent the first few minutes of my oral relating some gaffe my predecessor had made.

So my undergraduate days were over and, at that time, I could have gone straight into practice but for the need to do two years in one of the Services after doing six months in a local hospital appointment after the Finals examination. My choice had been the RAF and to my delight I was accepted. Mind you I was fairly confident of acceptance because of my spell as an ATC cadet during the war.

CHAPTER 4

National Service in the RAF: 1950-52

Having passed the Finals I then went on to do a house physician job in the Medical School for six months, which I really enjoyed. After this I was due for call-up to do my National Service for two years. However I had two cousins in Alberta, both married to doctors, who suggested that I should come out to Canada for a year instead. I found the idea appealing and so I contacted the authorities to see if I was allowed to defer National Service to which the answer was yes, but I would be liable for call-up on my return – unless I stayed away until I reached the age of 30. I therefore decided to do the Service stint first and I joined the RAF which proved a good choice especially as I was very fortunate regarding the places to which was posted.

Intake Course: RAF Moreton-in-the-Marsh: November 1950–February 1951

So I reported there in September 1950 for my intake course which was meant to introduce us to life in the RAF and what was expected of us as Service Medical Officers. From the outset we were ranked as Flying Officers in the first of our two years' service – equivalent to Lieutenant in the Army – while at the start of the second year we were promoted to Flight Lieutenant – equivalent to Captain in the Army. The group consisted of thirty doctors and five or six dentists, all of whom knew that they would never be doing any 'square bashing' i.e. marching on the parade ground – after the intake course. Yet for reasons best known to themselves the RAF authorities required us to do at least an hour's parading every day. This did not go down well with our group and when we marched back for lunch, led by the Warrant Officer (WO) and as he called a halt outside the Dining Room, he turned to find only about nine or ten of us in the squad. The others had just broken ranks and gone to their rooms en route. The WO was furious and tore us off a strip in what I can only call very colourful language.

Alas our standards of square bashing did not improve as much as expected and the main calamity came on the penultimate day. We had been taught the two salutes on the parade ground – 'squad on the march salute' and 'squad to the front salute' which involved halting, counting to four and then saluting. The squad was marching away from the WO whose voice did not carry particularly well when he gave the order. Those in front heard: 'Squad – salute!' and they thought the order was 'to the front' so they stopped, while those at the back, who were nearer to the WO, heard 'on the march' and they marched through the front of the squad. You can imagine the chaos, which provoked great hilarity in the group, a view not shared by the Warrant Officer, whose face was purple with rage and the air was blue with his obscenities.

Our group was judged to be beyond the pale and, as a result, we were excluded from the Passing Out Parade which hardly broke our collective hearts.

Next posting: RAF Colerne October 1950–February 1951

The intake course complete, we all had our first postings and there was always the risk of being sent to a small, dull station miles from anywhere, but I was sent to RAF Colerne. This was a state of the art, recently completed station near Bath with superb facilities. So, at the age of 24, I found that I had a batman to look after me i.e. to keep my room clean, iron my clothes, make the bed etc. I felt like a millionaire. He was a most pleasant and helpful young man with whom I had a very good relationship but one day he said that the batmen had been discussing their charges and they all agreed that I looked much too young to be an officer! This was just about the last thing I wanted to hear and so I decided to grow a moustache in an attempt to look bit older. It stayed in place for nine months but never succeeded in achieving the desired effect. The fact is that moustaches are meant for tall thin men with vertical heads where I failed on both counts.

Bath is a handsome city and it was a pleasure to go into the town at the weekends but I was only there from October 1950 until February 1951. Thus I never saw the city at its best especially as it lay in a basin of hills and had more than its share of winter fogs at that time.

The head of the Medical Unit at RAF Colerne was a Wing Commander who looked very tired and worn for his years when I first met him in his office. Several times he had the most terrible bouts of coughing. Each time he produced a bottle of what he called 'my linctus' and took a swig about which I had suspicions from the start. However since I am anosmic i.e. I have no sense of smell so I was not absolutely certain that it was alcohol. Later in the mess, fellow officers confirmed my impression and told me that he had survived a murder charge eighteen months earlier! His wife had been having an affair and he threatened her with a gun, which the jury felt might have gone off accidentally, and he was found not guilty. He knew however that his RAF career was over and indeed he was discharged while I was there.

Soon after I arrived at Colerne we had a formal Dining-in Night in dress uniform and since I knew few of my fellow officers I was a bit bored. Looking around I spied a large silver Quaich on the table which carried an inscription that I could not read. I therefore moved the Quaich slightly so that I could read the inscription more easily. At this point one of the officers leapt to his feet and addressed the President of the Mess Committee saying, 'I am sorry sir but the new doc. has handled the silver'. Unknown to me this was a punishable offence for which the offender might have to pay for a round of drinks, especially if he was very unpopular. However the PMC replied, 'Yes but F/O(Flying Officer)

Tulloch is new to RAF ways and so this punishment will not be implemented'. I sighed with relief as there were some 25 people at the dinner. I was never to make the same mistake again!

The new Wing Commander proved much more idiosyncratic than his predecessor or as the Officers' Mess put it he was 'mildly bonkers'. When I went to see him for the first time he was writing but did not look up as I entered and went on writing for 3-4 minutes before he addressed me. He then told me his name which he explained meant 'H- dancing around the Xmas tree'. I thought he was joking and laughed which only provoked a stern glare from the W/C. I sensed we were not going to get on and so it proved. He then told me that I was to do a locum at RAF Yatesbury, a centre for boy entrants to the RAF. I was warned it was a dull job as indeed it was. The work largely consisted of dozens of very brief physical examinations plus a similar number of inoculations and vaccinations. It may have been a dull job but it was very important work.

On my return from Yatesbury I was told that I was to go on a Tropical Medicine course at RAF Halton in Buckinghamshire. This pleased me, although I had asked to be posted to Germany, so that I could polish up the German I had learned at school. Halton turned out to be a magnificent Rothschild mansion and the course was a most interesting one. It was run by an outstanding Anglo-Egyptian pathologist and he was absolutely first class. In addition to being a distinguished tropical medicine specialist he was also an entomologist of international standing. I enjoyed the course very much indeed, as did my colleagues.

Then I returned to RAF Colerne and the one and only W/C H had already fallen out with the station commander, a Group Captain (equivalent of Colonel in the Army) and therefore his superior. Now it was a dictum in the services never fall out with an officer of higher rank, was not surprised when the G/C buttonholed me one evening in the mess and asked me how I was getting on with W/C H. I indicated that we were not a mutual admiration society and he was clearly not surprised. The G/C went on to mention that he too was having problems with the Wing Commander and that was as far as he went.

My final posting in the UK was a two-week spell to RAF Locking near Weston-super-Mare which had been an RAF Hospital during the war but it was now little more than the rump of a station. I was hard pressed to stretch my day's work out to two hours and I was bored stiff. Then I received a phone call from a secretary in our office at RAF Colerne telling me that I should have gone on embarkation leave three days earlier but the Wing Commander had forgotten to inform me. I rang him but he happened to be away for the day and so I decided to take action. I rang the Medical Officer for whom I was doing the locum and explained the circumstances. He immediately offered to return to his post- short term – so that I could go on embarkation leave instantly. Now in these circumstances one might have expected the W/C to be in apologetic mode on my return, for failing to send me on embarkation leave. However that was not his way and when I reported to him he snapped: 'Why have you deserted your post? If it was wartime you would have been shot!' He then stated that he would be submitting an Unfavourable Report on my conduct. To this I replied, 'In which case, Sir, I will report your failure to send me on leave on time which has cost me three days of the embarkation leave'. That silenced him and when I related the episode to the station commander he indicated that the adverse report by the Wing Commander would in any case have got no further than his office!

I spent the remainder of my embarkation leave at home with my parents in Dumfries and while there I received notice that I was being posted to the Suez Canal Zone in Egypt, which sounded to me very exotic. In addition, while all other members of my Tropical Medicine Class were flying to Suez, I was to get there by troopship which sounded less appealing. However I couldn't have been more wrong as the trip was a cruise from Liverpool stopping at Gibraltar, Malta and Cyprus en route to Suez. The weather was warm, the company was good and the food seemed excellent to me, especially when one bears in mind that food was still rationed in the UK at that time. Officers were required to wear dress uniform for dinner and when I came down in my – monkey jacket (slang for Officer Dress Uniform) I was astonished to find there were four courses on the menu – a new experience for me at that time – but not since! During the trip I offered to do a few surgeries to keep my hand in and the ship's surgeon was delighted to accept this offer. His office had been part of the Royal Suite and no other surgery I have seen in the past, or indeed since, was so luxuriously appointed. We were travelling on a liner called The Empress of Australia which had taken members of the Royal Family to the Antipodes in the thirties. After one surgery I had taken I decided to discuss a patient's condition with the ship's surgeon and when I knocked on his door it took some time for it to be opened. Then on admission I was aware that there was a girl in the next room hidden from view but neatly reflected in a mirror – it was the ship's nurse frantically combing her hair and still looking rather tousled. As I left the room the doctor put his fingers to his lips and said 'mum's the word'. The doctor and his nurse had been indulging themselves in a little harmless necking, as it was called in my student days, or so they claimed. However the Service disapproved of it on duty and I wasn't going to report a fellow Medical Officer.

 The trip took some ten days and officially we were not allowed to go ashore but in Valetta and Famagusta the ship's surgeon asked me to escort a sick patient who needed hospital care ashore. This enabled me to spend a couple of hours in each port including a visit to the castle ruin on which Shakespeare's "Othello " was partly based. Thence we sailed to Suez in the Egyptian Canal Zone.

RAF service in the Middle East 1951-52
The Egyptian Canal Zone 1951 – 1952 for nineteen months:
RAF Deversoir, my first posting in this Zone

When we reached Suez the start was hardly auspicious. I arrived to find that my name had been left off the arrivals list, the penalty for having a name starting with "T" and thus in the lower reaches of the alphabet. Indeed I was the last name on the list in this case. Mind you I must not moan since the same list location had enabled me to cruise to Suez while the others on the list merely flew – a much duller experience. However in this case I had no means of transport to RAF Deversoir, to which I had been posted. The sergeant responsible for transport seemed uncertain how to resolve this problem when suddenly a Humber Supersnipe swept in. This was a luxury vehicle at the time, reserved for the Royal Family or Senior Service Officers (Air Commodore and above) and the sergeant's face broke into a smile. He shouted to me: 'Hold on Sir, I'll get you in with the sky pilot', which did not mean anything to me so he added: 'You know Sir the "bible puncher" and then I realised that he was referring to the padre in RAF slang. In the Services at that time hilarious nicknames were two a penny among the other ranks. I found this most amusing until I discovered that doctors were known as 'quacks'. He was advising me that I was to travel in the air-conditioned Humber sent to collect an Air Commodore padre while my colleagues made the same trip in the back of two very uncomfortable Land Rovers with a canvas cover to protect them from the mid-day sun. The date of our arrival was May 6th, 1951, which happened to be the day on which the Egyptians expelled King Farouk and the Egyptian army took control of the country under General Neguib, who was a front man for Colonel Nasser. In due course, the latter took over the running of Egypt from the UK and for a time this caused instability, since the British feared that, if they lost control of the Suez Canal, this would create major problems for the British government.

RAF Deversoir, to which I was posted, was a fighter station based right at the point where the Suez Canal runs into the Great Bitter Lake in which we all did a great deal of swimming. There were three squadrons there – Numbers six, 213 and 249 – and the sixth rather saw itself as RAF aristocracy since they were one of the first block of fighter squadrons way back in 1918 when the RAF was first formed under Air Chief Marshall Sir Hugh 'Boom' Trenchard.

The other two squadrons took exception to this elitism and christened them 'the Sh-y Sixth'. They had to be on high alert most of the time and the highlight of their year was the trip to Mafraq in Jordan where King Hussein, who was strongly pro-British, treated the RAF like visiting royalty. It was the outstanding event of the year for the Jordanians, who turned out in large numbers to see the RAF give a splendid display of aerobatics. Finally, medals were issued to all the visiting personnel including the medical officers. I was very much looking forward to this event, but two or three cases of paratyphoid fever were diagnosed about a week before our departure and the RAF over-reacted and kept all doctors in the Canal Zone on station for a couple of weeks by which time our squadrons were already in Jordan. I was very disappointed to miss this 'mission' and meeting Hussein.

Deversoir was a very lively station but the problem was that there was scarcely enough work for one Medical Officer, much less two, and we soon became bored, especially as there was also a lack of female company. We seemed to spend a good deal of the time in the afternoons lying on the beach of the Bitter Lake and occasionally swimming out to wave to the passengers in passing liners.

Of course there was a reason for my under employment as I only did extra surgeries to reduce the burden on the Senior Medical Officer. However I was also warned that in the event of any of the three squadrons going 'on detachment' I was in the support team which went with them. During the time I was there no such detachment was required.

A flight in my first fighter jet aircraft

The highlight of my time on this station was when I first went up for a flight in a jet aircraft – a Gloster Meteor – normally a single seater fighter but this one had a second seat for training purposes. Before we took off he warned me that the acceleration on take-off was much more powerful than any other vehicle I may have used. Even so I was astonished by the violence of the engine pickup and the manner in which I appeared to be thrust backward into the squab of my seat on take-off. He finally asked if I would like him to do some aerobatics, which I accepted rather apprehensively, and he gave me a demo ending with a power dive. This proved quite exhilarating until near the end when I had a violent pain in my left ear which led me to believe that my eardrum had been ruptured. However when I put this to the Senior MO, who had much more experience than me in this field, he smiled and said that I was much more likely to have barotraumatic otitis and he proved to be correct. I had ruptured a blood vessel in my ear drum and was slightly deaf for ten days.

Request for a posting from RAF Deversoir

After four months of under-employment I was bored and decided to apply for another posting. I wonder, in retrospect, that I had the nerve, especially as the Postings Wing Commander said he had never had anyone seek a posting in under six months before. He asked then where I would like to go and I suggested Nairobi or Kyrenia in Cyprus but both posts had recently been filled. I then suggested Khartoum as history was one of my favourite subjects at school and I fancied myself travelling at last in the footsteps of Gordon, Kitchener, Churchill and the Mahdi, a great Sudanese rebel in the Victorian era. A second consideration was that I had been told that the social life there was very lively. He appeared astonished and said : 'I have never had anyone apply to go there before. It is hot as hell. However it falls vacant in two or three months and your name is on the ticket.' What he did not know was that the son of our family minister at home held a post in the Sudanese Colonial Service and he reported that the local lifestyle was very lively. Feeling rather pleased with the outcome I departed. It all seemed cut and dried but I hadn't allowed for the vagaries of Service life especially in the RAF.

RAF Shaibah – 'the hellhole of the RAF'

Some two weeks later I was wakened by an airman at about two a.m., who told me that I had two hours to get my day-to-day clothes together as I was being temporarily posted to RAF Shaibah near Basra in the middle of the Iraqi Desert. Now this Station was known in the Service as the hellhole of postings in the Middle East and the joke was that you were only sent to Shaibah if you had 'put up a black' (made a serious mistake). I was not aware of any such gaffe but I did wonder if the Wing Commander (Postings) in the Canal Zone had decided to teach me a lesson!

Two hours later I was being driven at top speed to RAF Fayid, the major station in the area, in a state of complete bewilderment. Why, I asked myself was I, a mere Flying Officer with no combat experience or specialist qualifications, being rushed out to Shaibah? However when I arrived at RAF Fayid, a major station at the lower end of the Bitter Lake, I was joined by three other medical officers – two the same rank as me and one a Squadron Leader. Of course we already knew that the Persians (as they were then known) had nationalised the Anglo-Iranian Oil Company without compensation which had led to the Abadan crisis. However, the general impression was that in due course an accommodation would be reached with the Americans interceding on our behalf. The fly in the ointment however was the truculent Persian leader Mossadegh who was making the most of his spell in the limelight. He was enjoying every minute of it and he would occasionally meet the press wearing only an expensive pair of silk pyjamas. At least that was what they looked like to me.

So we flew to Shaibah on July 22nd and were immediately told that the British Government were not confident that the Persians would protect British employees of the oil company who were being expelled. Thus we might have to invade the country temporarily to protect these families. If so, fighting was a distinct possibility and our task would be to set up a casualty station to deal with any injured personnel. In these circumstances we were warned that we might have to operate under fire. We all agreed that this filled us with a mixture of apprehension and excitement – more of the former!

However, it was not to be, for next day came the news that Averill Harriman, a prominent US statesman, had arrived in Tehran to begin negotiations. Harriman was a Democrat, businessman, politician and diplomat. He was pro-British and thus was very popular in the UK. So we were fairly confident that he would defuse the situation and so he did. Any intervention by us was first postponed for a week, then a further fortnight and finally indefinitely. However we had to stay in the Iraqi desert in the height of summer, with no work to do, although we did a number of locum surgeries voluntarily. To make matters worse the temperature rose over 100 degrees every day and the Persian Gulf has one of the highest rates of humidity in the world. A swim in the station pool was like a warm bath.

With too much time on our hands we soon became bored and problems arose from time to time, the worst of which concerned one of our quartet of doctors, Jerry Y****. He had borrowed the station ambulance to go to Smokey Joe's restaurant on the station at 10 p.m.(itself a serious offence to use an ambulance for this purpose) and on his way back he compounded his crime by demolishing about twenty yards of wall round the Sergeants' Mess in an attempt to avoid hitting a dog, the station mascot. Jerry's misfortune was further increased by the fact that the Station Commander was attending an event in the Sergeants' Mess and both parties had consumed a fair amount of alcohol. The result was that each had some difficulty in standing to attention with feet close together while the S/C dressed down Jerry and told him that there would be an immediate Court of Enquiry into his conduct.

At this point, as the roommate of the accused, I was summoned by the Station Commander and told that Jerry Y**** was my responsibility and that I had to ensure that he never left the camp. Since the station was surrounded by desert for hundreds of miles I had great difficulty in keeping a straight face when this order was issued.

Astonishingly the Court of Enquiry convened the following morning and the first question to Jerry was 'Why were you using the ambulance to visit the station restaurant at this late hour?'. Jerry's explanation was that his visit had been an attempt to check up on the restaurant's standards of hygiene by means of a surprise visit at a late hour. He added later that he had gone so far as to check all the meat in the restaurant's glass containers about which he claimed to have had some complaints. However he found no signs of poor hygiene. Thereafter there was a long session in the course of which the restaurateur was also questioned several times. He shrewdly confirmed Jerry's claims and in the end it was decided that Jerry had no charge to answer and a couple of days later he could be seen having a friendly drink with the S/C. Each of them, one felt, was highly satisfied with this outcome.

One of the most interesting and amusing episodes during my time in Shaibah was when I visited the local brothel, which was out of bounds to Service personnel. Thus it was visited several times each week by the RAF Police and the officer in charge invited me to join him on one of these visits. It was known locally as 'the Bullring' with 'the girls' all sitting round the perimeter and many of them seemed to be older than I had expected. Indeed a few looked to me the wrong side of 60 years of age. However there were also some pretty youngish girls. We were in a small group and I happened to be at the back when I felt my bottom being fondled by one of the older ladies whose smile revealed an impressive set of gums and one solitary tooth dangling loosely from her upper jaw. 'Oh that's Hetty. She makes advances to all the visitors I bring here,' said the RAF Police Officer taking us round.

Transfer to RAF Habbanya

Two months after I had arrived I found myself posted to this station which was said to be the largest air force station in the world at that time, but also in the middle of the Iraqi desert. It was remarkably well equipped with excellent accommodation and with no less than two swimming pools – one for officers and a second for other ranks. However this posting created a problem for me as most of my belongings were still in Deversoir, several hours flying time from Habbanya. I reported this problem to the Commanding Officer who replied airily, 'No problem there, Doc. Just hop a plane to the Canal Zone, collect your gear and return the same way. I'll see it is arranged" He was as good as his word and a couple of days later I found myself making the trip – it all seemed delightfully simple but alas I couldn't have been more wrong again.

When I arrived back to Deversoir I found a message awaiting me to say that they had an outbreak of paratyphoid fever and they would be short of doctors if this epidemic took off. Thus, under no circumstances was I to return to Habbaniya where, incidentally, all my day-to-day kit remained and it only caught up with me six months later. To my delight, I was also advised that when the epidemic was over I was to take up the promised appointment in Khartoum. They had even sent down a locum to keep the post warm for me. I had been less than just to the Wing Commander, Postings in Middle East Air Force HQ in Egypt, and there was more to come.

RAF Khartoum: A Happy Year 1951–52

In fact the parathyroid epidemic never developed and two weeks later I found myself flying down to RAF Khartoum where I was met by my locum who had not been at all keen to take on the posting. However by the time I arrived he was trying to stay there, fortunately for me, unsuccessfully. RAF Khartoum was one of the places used for tropical trials of new RAF aircraft to see how well they functioned in very hot conditions. The area had hot weather most of the time, especially in high summer, but, unlike Shaibah, the humidity was low. It was not a particularly busy station although it became busier when the tropical trials team joined us and not long after I arrived in the Canberra flew in for its tropical trials.

The Army had a hospital there which was used by all service personnel with some seven or eight doctors and rather more QAs (members of Queen Anne's Royal Nursing Service). By a remarkable co-incidence two of the doctors had been in my year at Aberdeen University. Looking back, I spent almost as much time at the hospital, especially in the evenings, as at the RAF Station, where the staff were young, fit and rarely ill. We saw an occasional malaria patient and also cases of dengue and sandfly fever and whenever possible I used the British Military Hospital to provide me with a reason for going there during the day. I also joined hospital rounds whenever possible to keep my hand in.

Landing on One Engine

Emergencies were very rare although we were usually called out when a plane was landing on one engine in both training programmes and emergencies. Nearly always this ended in a normal landing and as a result our staff in the medical centre became very bored by this work. Then, one day, we had a visit by an Air Vice-Marshall from Middle East HQ in the Canal Zone, who asked if he could have a flight so that he could see Khartoum from the air. He was to be accompanied by The Kaid, a British General who was C-in-C of the Sudanese Army. All went well with the flight until one of their engines cut out and they were obliged to land using only the other one. Of course, the pilots were fully trained in landing on one engine but nonetheless it is a bit frightening for passengers, to say the least. Now I was told that a normal landing occurs when the pilot is close to the ground and effectively he stalls the engine (called 'laying off'). On this occasion the pilot laid off rather too high and realising his error, turned up the power and managed to land normally the second time. Most pilots in the mess that evening thought it was a miraculous escape from a crash. When I went to see how the two Senior Officers were, I found them deeply shocked which was scarcely surprising. They had had the fright of their lives.

A Crisis in Wadi Halfa

Another strange episode began one Sunday morning when the Station Commander rang me up at 6 a.m. to report that an RAF serviceman had gone mad in Wadi Halfa, a bare godforsaken place on the Sudan Egyptian border. Wadi means watering place but there was precious little water there most of the year. It appeared that on the flight back to the UK his wife had informed him that she was leaving him for another man. This led to a noisy dispute between them on the plane in the course of which he was inconsolable and he threatened to commit suicide. So alarmed were the aircrew that they decided to land on an emergency airstrip at Wadi Halfa where they called the local police. The patient then escaped and tied himself to a railway line, but the police pointed out that the trains were some two or three days away. When the police released him, he attacked one of them who had to be admitted to hospital. Then he declared that he was going to drown himself, but once more the police told him there was a drought in WH at this time. Thereafter he appeared to settle down about half an hour before I arrived. I was to take one of my staff and we were to fly up to this place to sedate the Sergeant and escort him to the Canal Zone. He was also to be anchored to the seat on which he made the trip in case he tried to jump out of the plane. The Station Commander also told me that I would be met by the District Commissioner, who was coming in to take charge before I arrived.

On arrival I found two people awaiting me. The first was a very relaxed looking Englishman and the other was a native policeman. So I assumed I was speaking to the District Commander but in fact he was the patient and incidentally the D/C never appeared. I then told him that I had to escort him to the Canal Zone after he had been given a strong sedative. This he rejected outright and he held this line for about an hour by which time I was very frustrated and angry. I therefore told him bluntly that so far as I was concerned he could spend the rest of his life here in Wadi Halfa but he would not be leaving this spot without a sedative, a medical escort and anchored to a stretcher. I then turned to walk towards our Dakota (a popular troop transport at the time) and that did the trick. He agreed to have the injection and we flew him to Fayid without further mishap, where we were met by a psychiatrist whose behaviour seemed to me more idiosyncratic than our patient. He arrived with two friendly Alsatian dogs who kept jumping up on me and trying to lick my face while he made no effort to restrain them. He then told me they were police dogs and on a simple command from a policeman they could become aggressive which I hardly found reassuring. Eventually we got round to discussing the patient who then apologised for his earlier behaviour. Finally, I flew back to Khartoum and reported to the Station Commander who was very intrigued by the whole affair and pleased that the plane had not landed at RAF Khartoum.

The *possible* request for me to do a parachute jump (for which I had no training)!

I had a call one day from the Station Commander in which he told me that a plane was assumed to have crashed or crash landed south of Khartoum in an area to which access was not easy because of rocks, the last thing I would have expected in the Sudan. Thus one of my staff and I might have to be asked to do a parachute jump but the problem was that we had no training in this respect. We were then sent to the Parachute Officer who turned out to be a rather dour Midlander and whose first question was 'Have you ever jumped from a 15-foot wall as that is roughly the equivalent of the jolt you will get on landing from a normal parachute jump?'. I hadn't, to which he replied curtly, 'Pity' but my airman colleague claimed to have done it several times without mishap, which was reassuring. He then took us through the manner in which we must leave the plane and manage the jump. We were told to jump well clear of the aircraft although the risk of us being hit by the tail plane was very small! Then we would have some seconds in freefall after which we were to count <u>very slowly</u> from one to ten and then pull the ripcord. We were warned against panic and pulling the ripcord prematurely which would increase the risk of the chute not opening properly.

Finally he told us that there was likely to be a strong jolt at the point where the parachute opened and we should try to minimise the whiplash effect so far as possible by keeping our heads well back. Now the Parachute Officer was only doing his job in carefully briefing us as he did but his lugubrious manner and rather negative presentation seemed to aggravate our tension. We walked to the plane in silence only to be told that there would be a delay of about half an hour before we departed. In fact it was an hour and a half but then came the news that there had been no crash and the plane had landed safely. The problem was with radio connection. We did not have to make 'the jump' after all. I then did something I have never done before – I went to the Officers' Mess and had a very stiff whisky. Later I was told that the Parachute Officer was responsible for briefing other officers on parachute jumping and the Station Commander's duty was to ensure that he did it. Jumping out of a plane thousands of feet in the air was never an ambition of mine. However, paradoxically, when it was all over I felt a sense of regret, but not for long.

The year in Khartoum is one I look back on with real pleasure. The nurses and doctors had both been through demanding courses with a great deal of information to be absorbed, enabling them to pass the examinations. Both the Army and the RAF units were well staffed and so nobody was overworked. Thus we felt the time had come for us to enjoy ourselves. We worked from 7a.m. to 1 p.m., when we had lunch followed by a siesta in most cases, and then we retired to the Sudan Club. Service officers and nurses enjoyed the privilege of Club Membership and we swam there most days as well as playing tennis and squash. Usually we had our evening meal in the Mess but occasionally we would go out to dinner with the nurses at the Grande Hotel on the banks of the Nile – I can still hear the sound of the cicadas to this very day.

Sport is very important to the Services and I only realised this when another RAF officer and I won the Doubles in the Annual Khartoum Services Tennis Tournament. The Army, with far more competitors, had won every event for the previous 15 years and the RAF were delighted to beat them this time. Thereafter Fred – my tennis partner – and I were deluged with offers of short service or permanent commissions because the RAF believed that successful sportsmen made good leaders. The Service seemed much more interested in my skills as a tennis player than as a doctor.

Social life in Khartoum

Twice a year Officers were invited to the Governor General's Palace to a drinks party and we always went as the heads of all the communities in Khartoum were also invited and they brought their older sons and daughters with them. I recall one occasion when the head of a local community arrived with his wife and three daughters who were all simply gorgeous, if a trifle over made-up. Immediately the officers clustered around them like moths around a flame until the order went out that we had to mix more evenly with the other guests as well. One of the Army Officers began a clandestine affair with one of the daughters but when the army C.O. found out about the relationship he was quietly warned that it might have an adverse effect on his career.

Leave in Aden and a trip across the Sudanese Desert to Khartoum

Towards the end of my time in the Sudan I went on leave to RAF Aden along with Captain Rodney Wilkins (one of the Army Medical Officers) who had a doctor friend doing his National Service there. This was in 1952 and the place was entirely peaceful then. Our host found a room for us in the hospital where he worked and he ferried us around the town and surrounding country. It was a most enjoyable break. Then on the way back we stopped in Asmara which is a city about 10,000ft above sea level and virtually on the Equator so that the weather was much more temperate than we had anticipated. The result was a most enjoyable two days break there in conditions similar to high summer in England. While there we happened to run into a young couple who had just driven across the Sudanese desert from Khartoum in an open top Morris Minor, which had never been done before. I had met them socially in Khartoum and they asked me if I would like to join them on the way back. They stressed that they had equipment to meet all emergencies and the trip was to be made overnight. Souk lorries made the trip several times each week delivering supplies and we were to follow their tracks.

I was uncertain at first but in the end I agreed to join them with the blessing of my colleague Rodney. Then we drove through the mountains to the Sudanese border, taking the route followed by the British Army in 1941, when they fought and defeated the Italians Fascists. At one point we saw a boulder on which was etched the message 'Scotland for Ever', which was alleged to have been originally written in his own blood by a dying Scottish soldier during the fighting. We spent the night at the District Commissioner's house just inside the Sudanese border and at 4p.m. the following day we set out. The tracks of the Souk lorries were well marked and we had no difficulty in following them, but after an hour we ran into some very soft sand into which we gradually sank up to the axels. Jimmy D****** – the husband – said that there was no need to worry as he would soon get us out of this spot but when we tried the Morris simply sank deeper into the sand. Suddenly this had become more serious than anticipated as we had no tenting and at high noon the temperature would be over 100 degrees, although we had plenty of water. However, shortly afterwards four Sudanese appeared and Jimmy, a Colonial Officer, spoke to them in Arabic and explained our plight.

They were very tall, well-built men and they agreed to help, but it soon became clear that it was no easy job and they said they would prefer to do the work on their own. They then 'bumped' the car a short distance sideways themselves on several occasions but each time the car simply sank into the sand again as Jimmy tried to drive off. However at about the fifth attempt the wheels began to bite on a harder surface and to our great relief we were able to drive away. Thereafter we had no additional problems and we arrived in Khartoum about an hour later than anticipated. Only then was I informed that we were the first private car to make the trip and the authorities had advised against it as the Morris Minor was thought an unsuitable vehicle for the venture. There was unquestionably a degree of foolhardiness in what we had done and one wonders what the outcome would have been if the Sudanese had not happened to come along that evening when they did. However we did make the headlines in the local Khartoum paper.

Sole Fatal Accident

In the two years I served in the RAF I was only once called out to a fatal accident. A Sergeant Pilot in Iraq made a tragic error while doing unauthorised aerobatics and he crashed at something like 600 mph. I was sent out with another Medical Officer to retrieve his remains and I searched for ten to fifteen minutes before I found a warm trachea and upper bronchi. His body had been blown to pieces, which was hardly surprising. I recall thinking that this was part of a man who had been having breakfast in the Sergeant's Mess only thirty minutes earlier, blissfully unaware it was to be the last meal of his life. His entire remains fitted into a canister about the size of a large thermos flask. This was the most unpleasant experience of my entire time in the RAF and the other Medical Officer and I were close to tears as we thought of this family tragedy.

Historical figures in the Sudan

Another dimension of life in Khartoum which interested me, was travelling in the footsteps of the prominent figures already mentioned – twice. In particular I enjoyed visiting the site of the Battle of Omdurman where a small unpretentious metal sign recorded that the battle had taken place there and that it was thought to be the last cavalry charge of the British Army – a claim now contradicted by more modern research. This revealed that there were some cavalry charges in the early days of the Great War in

1914. I should add that General Gordon had always been a hero of mine from my schooldays, but these days historians, while recognising his bravery, have tended to regard him as a rather idiosyncratic figure. I also went to the Museum in Omdurman which proved most interesting and there, in the Visitor's book, was the signature of General Kitchener, as he then was – across two pages!

That year in Khartoum was most enjoyable, especially in the company of other doctors and nurses and I had a particular girl-friend there, but somehow we drifted apart on our return to the UK. Little did I think that fourteen years were to pass before I finally got down to proposing for the first time.

I departed from Khartoum in September 1952 and flew back to the UK having completed my two years National Service in the RAF. I had enjoyed every minute of it and now I moved to pastures new after a short break at my parents' home in Dumfries. I was just recovering from bacillary dysentery and had lost a stone in weight which alarmed my mother who insisted that I go to bed for three days to aid my recovery and take egg and sherry 'as a tonic'. Poor mother – her views on medical care were mediaeval, gloriously unscientific and they remained so even after I had qualified as a doctor. Of course I recovered quite quickly, as I was young and fit then. Mother was delighted and she drew my attention to the benefits of her 'tonic' which I felt had had nothing to do with my recovery. In fact it tasted foul and I only took the tiniest sip while she was there and as soon as she departed I decanted the remainder down the drain.

CHAPTER 5

Postgraduate Training in Worcester: 1952-54

House Physician: General Medicine – Worcester Royal Infirmary 1952/53 for six months

Since I remained single I decided to devote two years to hospital jobs in various disciplines as I prepared for general practice. This took me to Worcester Royal Infirmary, where I worked for a General Physician with a special interest in diabetes, a disease in which I had developed a special interest. Even the history of diabetes and the discovery of insulin seemed fascinating to me, not least since one of the four discoverers – Professor John Mcleod – was a graduate of my own medical school in Aberdeen. Incidentally most people believe that Banting and Best alone discovered insulin, whereas the reality is that they discovered an impure form of insulin, which worked in animals but proved ineffective and toxic in human beings. However a very capable biochemist from Calgary – Professor Bertram Collip – soon purified the extract which proved effective and non-toxic in human beings. However Banting and Best then went to the Canadian press and presented themselves as the discoverers of insulin and the myth stuck. Even the Nobel Committee showed poor judgement in awarding the Nobel Prize to Mcleod and Banting alone and ignoring Best and Collip, who had done most of the terminal scientific work. Best never forgave them for this error but he went on to have the most distinguished career of the quartet. I also recall his textbook, which was a success on both sides of the Atlantic. I read it myself and found it excellent. I can even recall the title seventy-four years after I bought the book – 'Medical Physiology' by Best and Taylor. Physiology, by the way, covers the normal function of the body while pathology does the reverse.

I went on to enjoy the six months as a house physician which gave me a sound grounding in general medicine. The consultant was a pleasure to work for and he was an excellent clinician, but he always talked as if he was hard up. This was a result of educating his family at an expensive public school but his income must have been substantial as he had a thriving private practice while his wife was also working as a GP. In addition, he drove a very expensive car, no doubt to impress his private patients. So when he said one day that he had to think twice before buying a new pair of shoes I found this hard to accept. However, I admired him, especially when he told me that he had passed his MRCP[1] at the first attempt in what was and is a very difficult examination. Bill Cranston, the most talented student in my year at Aberdeen University, did likewise and so did the late Roger Bannister, with whom I used to play golf occasionally.

House Surgeon: Obstetrics–Ronkswood Hospital Worcester 1953 for six months.

Later, I moved on to my second appointment as house surgeon where I was working for a Scottish obstetrician – Mr Chalmers – who proved an ideal 'chief' as we called them. He was very keen on his 'difficult deliveries and the best way to handle them was with the House Surgeon on hand. Occasionally we found that it was impossible to deliver the baby by the vagina and a Caesarean Section was required. I helped at these and they invariably came off successfully. This was the most enjoyable of the three Worcester sessions and I sat the Diploma in Obstetrics just after I had finished. I had been briefed by a friend who was an Obstetric Registrar on the fact that Examiners in Obstetrics

---

1 MRCP is Membership of the Royal College of Physicians and the examination is very difficult to pass at the first attempt

loved questions on the subject of forceps and I was pleased to find two different forceps on the table at the Viva Examination. However the Examiner paid no attention to them until late in the day and just as he raised the forceps to put a question on them a bell rang and the Viva (known as an Oral in Scotland) was over and I had passed.

Towards the end of this session as his HS, Mr Chalmers took me aside and asked me whether I wanted to be an obstetrician or not. I replied that it was the only speciality I had ever considered but I could not face its bedfellow – gynaecology.

A trip up the Amazon

There was a hiatus of ten weeks at Worcester before my third session as a Resident Surgical Officer (Senior House Officer) began and I managed to fit in a trip up the Amazon as a ship's surgeon with the Booth Line, sailing from Liverpool. Apart from the cargo this small liner delivered to Brazilian ports, it also collected poor Portuguese from Lisbon & Oporto emigrating to South America. These were the days when only the affluent and the really rich could afford to depart on a cruise; even a modest one. In the case of this trip, the ship was British and it was used for trading primarily, coupled with ferrying the poor Portuguese to South America especially Brazil. Sometimes they were successful but more often they were not and they knew it was a gamble. As we left Oporto the relatives burst into tears followed by weeping and wailing audible for at least an hour since they feared they would never see their relatives again as was often to be the case. It was really a very moving experience.

In addition we had some twenty English passengers, all well-heeled. I recall that one was managing director of a British airline; secondly we had a middle-aged divorcee who wore sunglasses even if the sun was not shining. She also claimed to be a close friend of the novelist Somerset Maugham via her father, who was a judge. Then there was a rather jolly American who spent much of his time at the bar. He also regarded himself as a bit of a comedian. One day he asked me if the stethoscope was used much in venereal disease which seemed an odd question for a lay person. When I had answered the question, he replied 'Really, I thought you might use it to listen for "the clap" – ha ha ha'. He could be amusing but he overplayed his cards occasionally.

Finally there was another American who had just retired as Director of an Aeronautical College in Brazil. His wife had recently divorced him and it had clearly been a costly affair. He was not on the ship from the outset but joined us at the estuary of the Amazon, initially just to look round the ship. Then he decided that he would like to make the trip up and down the Amazon River and he said to me, 'Come and see how things are done in Brazil.' So we went to the booking office where he asked if there was any free accommodation on the ship to which the response was 'Sorry sir, none whatsoever. The Yank then produced a ten cruzeiro note and openly handed it over inside the passport to the employee who, without a hint of embarrassment, offered him the choice of several rooms. 'That is the way they do things in Brazil,' said the Yank, as he came across to me.

Another interesting party was a single middle-aged lady who kept talking endlessly about her investments. This caught the ear of the Yank and he began courting her but it turned out she was much less wealthy than she had suggested, which led to the affair being ended two years after they were married, I found out about this from fellow travellers after the trip.

Each morning I held a surgery, followed by the captain's tour of inspection of the ship and I was struck by the primitive nature of the accommodation and working conditions for the ordinary seamen, but this was 1954 and I am sure that things are much better today. The Captain seemed a very conscientious man and every day he asked me about the health of the crew.

The food was of good quality by the standards of the day when you realise that post war rationing was just coming to an end and cases presenting in the sick quarters were more likely to be due to trauma rather than disease among the crew. I could hardly complain that I was overworked, for most of the crew were relatively fit young men. However there were problems with a schizophrenic who had concealed his illness when applying for his post. He kept complaining that he was hearing voices coming over the ventilation system on the ship and things became so bad that we had to offload him in Barbados, especially as he was threatening to kill himself. When a passenger did turn up, the commonest complaint was diarrhoea, often mild and easily manageable – nature did the curing and I got the credit.

We happened to reach Bridgetown, capital of Barbados just before New Year's Eve. There I met a doctor called Dingwall, who had been in the year below me at Aberdeen University, although I did not know him well. Nonetheless, he invited me to a New Year's Eve Party which started in the hospital in which he worked and from which we made our way by boat to three or four ships anchored offshore. My tolerance of alcohol has always been poorer than average, which is why I have always been a very modest drinker. However on this tour of the ships it was hard to control drinking and I wound up mildly intoxicated which led to me falling asleep on a strange ship. The problem was that our ship was due to depart on the following day and I had become detached from the rest of my party. However a message was sent to my ship and the Captain sent a launch to collect me. He was less than impressed by my state of mild intoxication despite the fact that he was *very* mildly intoxicated himself! Mind you the ship was anchored just offshore for this New Year's Eve party and the Captain and I both had to be sober for our respective duties the next day, and we both were.

We then sailed towards the mouth of the Amazon in which there seemed to be a number of islands of varying sizes which had been created by silt washed down from the main body of the river. Here the Captain had to sail the ship through sometimes narrow channels, which were, in some cases, remarkably shallow, with the result that both the bottom and the sides of the hull were scraped several times by the sandy base of the river, without any damage being done. The estuary is about 150 miles wide but it narrows to about eighty miles across in the Lower Amazon and, since all the liners keep to one side of the river especially when sailing upriver, one was often unable to see the other bank. At that time –1954 – the banks were nearly always heavily wooded. There are said to be almost one hundred different races in this part of the river and a minority of them live in homes on stilts by the banks of the Amazon. It was thought then that some of them in the remoter parts of the jungle may never have made contact with civilised races such was the density of the Brazilian jungle at that time.

We stopped at several cities in the lower Amazon to deliver goods and were struck by the poverty and poor quality of life of the native people living there. We were told later that the gap between rich and poor in Brazil is very wide and we were encouraged to bring books, pencils, pens and stationery as in most areas there is a lack of funds even for such basic requirements. The basis of this problem is corruption in a country with vast natural resources and an economy which should be booming but isn't. Furthermore, when I returned on a cruise to Manaus almost sixty years later there was little sign of improvement. Even today – 2020 – the President of Brazil is quite likely to be impeached over financial irregularities in the near future. Yet in the late Victorian era this was an area of great financial wealth, largely based on the rubber boom at the turn of the century. This is reflected in the mansions built for owners and even more so, in the magnificent Opera House in Manaus.

Sadly for the Brazilians, a British agent smuggled a boatload of rubber saplings out to Malaya where the industry was run more efficiently, thus making the British Empire the world's greatest rubber producer at that time. It also ruined the Brazilian rubber industry.

Currently the area around Manaus is also said to contain the greatest plant and animal areas in the world, which has led to steadily increasing numbers of tourists in recent years. The trip up the Amazon was really a working holiday abroad and, as a result, it gave me a taste for travel which was to enrich my life in years to come.

Back to Ronkswood Hospital Worcester as a Senior House Officer in Surgery 1953–54

On my return to Ronkswood I started my year as Senior Surgical Officer working with a Consultant who liked even his most junior staff to undertake surgical operations which they felt competent to handle – under his supervision at first, of course. Now I had no ambition to be a surgeon but I was quite keen to undertake minor surgery e.g. appendicectomies, hernias, trauma etc. So after I had assisted at about six appendix removals I was allowed to do the surgery, with the Consultant next door if required. All went well and it really was a quite simple procedure. There was an incision of at least 4–5 inches over the appendix[2], after which one raised a loop of large bowel from within the abdomen with a series of lines running down them called the 'taenia coli'. At or near the end of these lines the appendix was to be found, removed and a purse-string suture inserted. It was all delightfully simple and the first time I did the operation, assisted by a nurse only, but with the consultant in the next room, it went like dream. Alas, the second time around was less straight-forward, for when I went to the end of the taenia there was no sign of an appendix or at least I could not find one – to my dismay. I had been unlucky enough to encounter an ectopic appendix underneath the bowel instead of being in its usual position on top – a rare finding. In the course of my year in this appointment I must have done some fourteen appendicectomies at least without ever seeing another ectopic. Looking back now, I got on well with the Consultant and it was a most enjoyable year, but surgery was not for me. I then did one locum in a practice in the Midlands and thus my general practice career had begun – or so I thought.

---

2 These were the standards of the day. Today surgeons would have a fit if the house staff did that. They make a tiny incision, insert a narrow tube through which they operate and the recovery time is much shorter.

CHAPTER 6

Starting General Practice in Coventry: 1954–63

At this point in 1954 a major problem arose which I should have anticipated but didn't. I did not realise that there were so many applicants for each post, and of course I had the additional handicap of being unmarried, the importance of which I had also underestimated. Wives in those days were on call with their husbands i.e. they handled calls when the doctor was already out on another call. As a result when I applied for a post, in the majority of cases I did not even get a reply. The minority who did reply included one which read.Thank you for your application received together with 140 others. This post has now been filled." Worse still, I was not at this point in a serious relationship with a girl who might have met my requirements. I did have some interviews but it soon became obvious that unmarried applicants had little chance of being offered any decent post.

My morale was particularly low and I even considered emigrating to Canada or Australia, which would have broken my parents' hearts – I am an only son, although I had a sister nine years younger than me. At this point, to my surprise, I was offered interviews for two posts in Coventry and Walsall and each practice offered me a partnership. I decided to accept the former because it was a two-man practice and the other partner said he was retiring in a couple of years which would leave me as senior partner. He was a very nice old boy who had been obliged to look after 6000 patients in Coventry throughout the Second World War and the strain had left its mark. He looked old for his years although he was to live into his nineties. When I asked about the rota arrangements he replied: 'We don't have an out of hours rota in this practice. You can go out whenever you want This implied that he would provide cover while I was out. It also meant that I was on call every night and also when I returned from any social outing. However I was young and I felt I could cope with this for two years until he retired, when I would become senior partner. We always got on well working together despite the fact that, like most doctors coming to the end of his career, he was no longer up to date. However, his experience, nonetheless, proved valuable to us both when thalidomide became available and he advised me not to use it in the short term although it had been recommended for use in pregnancy originally. I accepted his advice and the result was that we had no cases of phocomelia – deformed or absent limbs – so far as I can remember I was also allowed to use the flat above the surgery at a concessional rate and the couple who looked after the building, were responsible for dealing with calls when I was out. All went well until the end of two years when he advised. me that he had decided to defer his retirement 'a little longer' – in fact he stayed on for another seven years. This unsettled me and I began to consider other alternatives and among the applications I made was one to a private practice in Westminster at the request of my girlfriend at that point. Prima facie it looked interesting as his patients included MPs of all political parties, celebrities, a few aristocrats and sportsmen. However I was then voting for the Labour party and I had idealistic objections to my being involved in private practice but I was interested in seeing how private general practice compared with NHS practice. The interview consolidated my views, especially as the practice did not handle obstetrics or paediatrics, the parts of medicine which most interested me most at that time. Indeed I was about to take the examination for a post-graduate diploma in obstetrics. Still I departed asking the doctor to let me know if he felt I was suitable – merely out of interest – and then I would make my mind up. I also asked him to mark the letter 'Private as I did not want my partner to open it. When one of us was away on holiday the other opened all mail unless it is marked Private'.

I happened to be away for the weekend the next week and when I returned I found that the senior partner had opened the unmarked letter and was very concerned by the contents. I then told him that, after five years, I was finding the burden of doing so many hours duty on top of routine daytime work very hard to cope with. He immediately responded by offering me every Saturday off duty from 11a.m., when the surgery ended, till Sunday night when I returned to the flat. This was a crafty move on his part as the rate of calls in this weekend period was usually lower than average and my out of hours duties were unchanged unless I was away on Saturday night. Still I accepted the offer as a gesture of goodwill.

When I first entered general practice I was dismayed to find that around a quarter of the problems presented were trivial and could have quite easily been dealt with by a nurse along with GP back-up if required. I therefore decided to find an area of general practice in which the standards of care needed improvement and after six months I decided to choose medical records. After all, I argued, there are few enterprises in which man is involved that cannot be improved by a first-class record system and the one taught at medical student level was designed for use in hospital.

In general practice at that time progress notes and letters from other sources were kept in 'files' which were really cardboard envelopes measuring 8 ½" by 6 ½" originally introduced in 1908 by Lloyd George. The contents of these files were rarely properly indexed and the progress notes and reports were virtually never arranged in chronological order as an index. Neither was important material such as drug sensitivity and serious illness regularly highlighted, while the progress notes often completely lacked structure. Thus the files were a poor source of reference and utterly obsolete in an era when the reports arrived in a variety of notepaper sizes. Yet a significant minority of GPs fought to retain them because they could be fitted into the pocket of an overcoat.

None of these files met the basic requirements for a medical record file i.e. a summary of important past medical history, with progress notes and reports from other quarters arranged in chronological order. In addition important material in the progress notes needed highlighted by underlining. The benefit of this was that every new problem presented by the patient could be seen at a glance in the context of the previous medical history and important diagnoses were highlighted to make them an easy source of reference. Over the next two years I converted all my files to the A4 format and in addition I highlighted important findings in the progress notes. Here the credit must go to another GP, Irvine Loudon, who had been instrumental in persuading the Department of Health (DoH) to convert to the A4 format record system. He was a friend of mine and he managed to persuade the DoH to let me have a full set of the new system when he knew I was keen to convert the entire practice to this format. Finally I prepared a summary of important previous medical history in each case. As a result I was able to review every problem presented in this context at a glance and I found this most helpful in handling a patient in the brief period we had for consultation. In the meantime my senior partner expressed an interest in the new system and he asked if I would convert his files to the new format, which I did over the next two years. I shall return to this later as the decision to take a special interest in records was to alter my career radically.

Finally my Senior Partner retired in 1963 and I appointed Dr John Sutherland, a fellow graduate of my own Medical School, Aberdeen University, joined as a junior partner. He had been recommended to me and he proved to be an excellent choice so I assumed that I would complete my career working with him.

CHAPTER 7

Change to a practice in Bicester: 1963–87

However, one evening in October of the following year I had a phone call from Dr J F*****, an old friend from our University days, with whom I had kept in touch. In fact I often spent a weekend with him and his wife in my bachelor days during which he and I found common ground on the manner in which the NHS should develop in the future. He was ringing to say that his partner had advised him that he planned to retire in six months and he invited me to come down to take his place in the Bicester practice. At first I thought he was joking since I was senior partner on a good salary which would drop by some £4,000 if I were to join him and this was a large sum of money in 1963. I asked for a week to consider the offer by which time he had sweetened the pill by offering me a much better deal than he would have offered any other doctor joining the practice. Even then it was a difficult decision for I was quite happy practising in Coventry along with J Sutherland. A move to Bicester in partnership with Dr J F***** and his sister-in-law was always going to be something of a gamble for a canny Scot. So I discussed the matter with a colleague whose opinion I respected and he advised me strongly to make the move, pointing out that I would have one of the best medical schools in the UK on my doorstep and the quality of consultant support would inevitably be better than in Coventry at that time. I took his advice and have never regretted doing so. So in September 1963 I went to live in a cottage in Middleton Stoney some three miles from Bicester and quickly settled down in practice with my two new partners. I was still a bachelor and I was not destined to meet my wife until some two and a half years later. The practice was a busy one with Bicester growing steadily larger and there were only two practices in the town at that time.

So we were obliged to double the size of the practice building. In addition to British patients there were still some two thousand central European natives, many of them from Serbia or Croatia, who had fought with General Mihailovic against Marshall Tito, who was supported by the Russians. Others were from Russia, Poland and Hungary and their crime was that they had fought against the Russians either as guerrillas or with the Nazis. Most of them had a visceral hatred of the Russians, even more than the Nazis in many cases. They were described locally as "European Voluntary Workers" and were involved in often menial work at the Central Ordnance Depot. They knew, of course, what their fate would be if they went back to their home countries in the mid-sixties. Another twenty-five years were to pass before they could safely make that trip. Many of the men became reasonably fluent in English but the women, even after twenty years in this country, often knew no more than a few words of English. You can imagine the issues this created when they had problems in their private parts, as the husbands' command of English was overstretched. However as I got to know them better our relationship became more relaxed and occasionally I would be favoured with a smile. They were a sad people, displaced from their homelands to which they would have loved to return, but they knew that this was impossible, at least for the time being. Much later they were able to go back but by this time in many cases their offspring had married British subjects, so that in the end they often returned to live in the UK.

The move to Bicester proved a success from the outset as the practice was well organised and the hospital service in Oxford proved outstanding. However I had to go through all 1900 files of the patients on my list and reset them to the Problem Oriented Medical Record system (POMR) which I had developed in Coventry, based on a system in the USA. This involved indexing all the files, structuring the progress notes by underlining important material which made the records a much better source of reference. In addition I developed forms which linked the findings graphically in such conditions as hypertension and diabetes so that one could review the past 3-4 years findings at a glance. This facilitated the continuing review of these chronic diseases and was later to prove very important in the computerisation of records. I had read an article on this subject in which the author emphasised the vital importance of the data being fully structured. I knew full well that few record systems were more unstructured than in medicine at that time – the sixties – and this criticism applied equally in hospital and general practice. In both fields file contents rarely had an index or summary of important contents and highlighting of these findings was only done in a minority of cases. One may well imagine how poor the records were as a source of reference in a busy surgery and how difficult it would be to computerise such unstructured data. For me the main benefit was that the records were much better organised and every new problem could be seen in the context of the previous medical history, which at times proved very important.

In addition each problem was graded for severity as follows:
- undiagnosed problem – broken pencil line
- provisional diagnosis – solid pencil line
- final diagnosis – solid dark line
- serious illness – solid blue line
- terminal illness – solid red line

I also devised a flow chart which displayed data in a progressive graphic rather than numerical form that facilitated review of chronic disorders like diabetes and hypertension.

CHAPTER 8

Marriage to Christine Goffe: 1966

At this point of my life I was heading for forty and still single. There was a girlfriend but it was a relationship going nowhere yet again and then one Sunday I went to visit her only to find that she was about to go and help a friend with some task. She suggested that I should stay at her flat until she returned and I could pass the time reading her Sunday newspaper. Alternatively she suggested I could go and have chat with a girl called Christine Goffe who lived in the same house just a few doors down the passage. She was engaged to be married to a doctor who was doing a house job in a Midlands hospital where the workload was heavy. He had come down for the weekend and having worked long hours he was dead tired and apparently he had spent most of the visit asleep as a result. In view of this I decided not to visit Christine at first but later, fortunately, I changed my mind. Had I not done so I suspect the outcome would have been quite different. I was rather taken with her quiet diffident charm, coupled with a lively sense of humour and I remember thinking that that her fiancée would be a lucky man. I departed, never expecting to see her again but what I did not know was that their relationship was winding down since they had both begun to have reservations as to whether they were made for each other. In due course the engagement was broken off and by this time my own affair had also ended. However, I did not find out until some weeks afterwards and I decided not to contact her for a few weeks to enable her to unwind from what must have been a traumatic experience. However I couldn't bear to wait and I invited Christine out to dinner some three weeks later. Then some three months thereafter we were engaged with strong parental approval on both sides, to my relief. I recall asking Christine afterwards whether she was concerned about the seventeen years difference in our ages and her reply has become a family joke. I think she meant to say that she wished the gap wasn't quite so wide but instead she did say, wish you were not quite so old ! And that was a little matter of fifty odd years ago!! It has been a marriage which has given us both enormous pleasure. Neither of us was ever volatile and we have never had a real row but we did have one dispute over which of two houses we should buy and neither of us was prepared to give way. So the only answer was to look elsewhere. Stability and flexibility in any marriage are very important factors.

We spent our honeymoon in Madeira in perfect weather conditions and I must say I am sure that there is no girl in the world who would be more suitable for me than Christine – the ultimate accolade. I had 'got it bad' to use the jargon and she seemed equally keen. I need hardly say that the nature of the developing relationship tended to confirm our initial impressions. Thus the marriage has been a very successful one – well worth the wait and it also produced a daughter and two sons all of whom are in business and thriving. My only disappointment was that none of them chose medicine, but in addition I have four granddaughters one of whom plans to be a surgeon. I also have one grandson who might prove to be the last of this line of Tullochs. So I shall be advising that a few sons and one daughter are the order of the day.

Alistair and Christine on their wedding day 26 November 1966

Christine and Alistair in Argentina in the late 1990s

CHAPTER 9

GP Research Appointment: 1967–87

In the Summer of 1967, I went along with the family on holiday in Scotland and I fitted in a refresher course at Aberdeen University. While there I met Roy Weir, who had been in my year when we were students, once again. He was Senior Lecturer in Community Medicine in the Medical School and had recently published an article on medical records in the British Medical Journal. I told him that I had enjoyed the article and that I was interested in medical records and the manner in which they needed to be improved. He then told me that he was looking for a GP specially interested in records and he immediately offered me an appointment as a full-time Lecturer in Community Medicine. I was tempted, but later I decided to refuse the offer as I did not want to give up general practice and I had just become Senior Partner. He then advised me to contact Dr Donald Acheson, then the May Reader in Medicine and a rising star in this field, of whom we shall hear more later. He had been doing work on Record Linkage (RL) and was looking for a practice in the area to work with him on this subject. I should mention at this point what RL involves. The oldest example was the temperature chart which has been in use since at least 1880. Put "temperature chart" in Google and you will see a bewildering number of examples. The underlying concept was that if clinical findings were scattered throughout the progress notes they did not express their message clearly and the answer was to link the findings e.g. blood pressure, biochemical findings etc. together in a chart. This chart corrected the lack of clarity and the records expressed their message much more clearly in a graphic rather than numeric form. For some reason the medical profession has always ignored this principle and left their findings in chronic diseases such as hypertension and diabetes unlinked. This results in a cross-sectional view based primarily on the findings at the latest consultation whereas with a flow chart the assessment enables the doctor to survey the last few years' findings at a glance, which is likely to enable him or her to assess progress more accurately. On the other hand other professionals such as epidemiologists, economists, bankers and stockbrokers do not make the same mistake. I designed a flow chart for hypertension which we used in the practice. Then Dr Acheson offered the practice two sessions which were obviously intended for me as I had done all the research work on records.

However the senior partner who had not been involved in this work in any way insisted that he was taking both sessions. I was most upset about the unfairness of this behaviour, especially as we were close friends. However I felt confident that Dr Acheson would ask why I, who had done the research and made the original contact with him, was not involved. However he did not take this action and it was a decision they were both to regret. I, too, was disappointed not to be involved in working with Acheson. About a year later Dr Acheson was asked to take on the task of establishing a new Medical School in Southampton and he asked John if he would establish and develop the Department of Primary Care, Dr Acheson's name for a new form of general practice which never developed so far as I am aware. However, in fairness, John seemed to have developed the General Practice Training Programme and established the Department satisfactorily which was a difficult task, especially as he had not been through the academic mill. He confided to me before he left the practice that he did not enjoy lecturing or research, a considerable disadvantage for a doctor taking on the running of an Academic Department. Then after a few years he became disenchanted and developed a personal problem. We had been friends since our medical student days and I think he felt guilty about the way he had treated an old friend since, after 7-8 years, the Xmas cards stopped coming, he broke off all communication and he even stopped coming to see my wife and me when visiting the Bicester area. It was a sad end to the whole affair and the irony is that if John had not intervened I might well have been offered the post at Southampton although I am quite certain that I would have refused it. Fast tracking anyone into a senior academic post with a lack of academic experience is a recipe for trouble. Indeed years later when Oxford University decided to found a Department of Public Health and General Practice, my partners and some other colleagues thought that I would apply for this appointment, especially as I was the only GP in the Oxford area with an academic appointment already at that time. In fact I did not apply as I did not see myself as academic material and I have never regretted that decision. There were at least two or three people who were really bright in the Oxford area and I expected them to apply for the post. In the end it went to a friend of mine, Dr Godfrey Fowler who was successful in establishing the Department of Public Health and Primary Care.

However, there was one bonus for me on John's departure. Since Dr Acheson was departing and there was little sign of the Record Linkage Project being continued, I feared that the appointment would be terminated. However, Oxford University, which did not at that time have a Department of General Practice, decided that the appointment should continue as there was insufficient research being done in general practice in the Oxford area at that time. At first I was left in limbo i.e. unattached to any Department, and later I was temporarily attached to the Regius Department of Medicine in the University, pending the development of the Department of Public Health and Primary Care, although I was never on the staff there. I was merely temporarily attached to this department.

At that point some 18 months after John's departure, about the time when computers were just coming over the horizon in general practice, I read an article on the computerisation of medical records. This paper was at great pains to emphasise the need for records requiring computerisation to be 'fully structured' in order to facilitate data input. I immediately recognised that nothing was less structured than GP record files in the National Health Service at that time. The Lloyd George record envelope was out-of-date and quite inadequate. In most files the letters were at that time rarely even filed in chronological order. Finally progress records rarely showed any sign of structure as important findings were rarely highlighted, while the medical conditions were never graded for severity. At this point I contacted the Department of Health to draw their attention to this important problem and here I had a stroke of luck. The person to whom I spoke had read another article on the same subject elsewhere which also emphasised the importance in data input of *structured* records and he was hoping to devise a system which would resolve the problems of the current unstructured record system and make computerisation easier. This would involve the employment of a research nurse for two to three years and the cost would be £7,500 per annum for three years but I emphasised that, if the system was implemented nationally, the introduction of computerisation might be greatly facilitated. I knew that there was a Small Grants Fund for research in general practice which I hoped to tap for this purpose. However I was far from optimistic that my application would bear fruit and when I discussed the matter with colleagues they shared my view. However, much to my surprise, the Department of Health accepted my offer and the funds were granted. Naturally I was delighted, primarily because I felt that a carefully designed record system in general practice would improve clinical care, teaching, research and epidemiology. In addition, the reduction in cost of data input would be considerable. Even the speed of input would be increased greatly.

CHAPTER 10

Nuffield Travelling Research Fellowship in the USA: 1972

At this point –1971 – I applied for a Nuffield Travelling Research Fellowship to visit American centres using the Problem Oriented Record System (POMR) which I proposed to modify for use in the National Health Service. I was awarded the Fellowship and decided to spend half of my time based at the Rochester Medical School in New York State near the Canadian border, one of the best medical schools in the USA. In addition, I was to visit medical centres across America and Canada. I decided that Christine and the family were to accompany me on the first half of the trip after which they would return to the UK.

We flew from Heathrow across the Atlantic to Chicago and then on to Denver in the Rocky Mountains (known in the USA as the "The Mile High City") and from there we flew down to Flagstaff, Arizona so that we could see the Grand Canyon, which can only be described as awesome. It is a massive rent, or more accurately, series of rents in the surface of this land in Arizona, creating canyons through which the mighty Colorado River flows thousands of feet below. The reaction of anyone seeing these canyons for the first time is often to be struck silent by a sight unmatched anywhere else in the world. It seemed to me like a cross-section of time as we looked at the many layered cliffs. Everyone who can afford the cost of a trip to Arizona should see this magnificent sight.

From Flagstaff we flew to San Francisco (Frisco to most Americans) a city of great character with its cable cars, magnificent bridge, extraordinary microclimate and enormous stately sequoia trees nearby. We also found the people remarkably warm-hearted and helpful. When we took the children into a restaurant, the waitresses always rushed to get 'boosters' and a high chair to bring them up to table level – without being asked.

Then one day as we walked the children along a pavement in the city a woman came up to me and said gravely, 'Myyyy (pause for dramatic effect) what beautiful children you have'. Now our children were attractive, vivacious and entertaining and we were very proud of them, but we had rarely thought of them as beautiful – still as they say, beauty is in the eye of the beholder. I therefore thanked her and she replied with a question: 'are you English?' Now, when asked that question wherever I am, I always pretend, as a Scot, to be mortally offended by being taken for an Englishman. However she did not recognise that I was only joking and responded with a heartfelt apology! I remember thinking I must mend my ways.

The next stop was Seattle and then Vancouver. These were two handsome cities and by this time I was beginning to realise that their medical record systems were not that different from ours in the UK and in several cases they had never even heard of Problem Oriented Medical Records. From Vancouver we drove through the Rocky Mountains, which were again very imposing, to Calgary, the capital of Alberta where I had two female cousins. One was married to a GP surgeon in Calgary and the other to a paediatrician in Edmonton who subsequently became President of the Canadian Medical Association. There we had a get together of the MacKenzie Clan – my mother had four brothers, two of whom emigrated to the USA a few years before the First World War and later moved on to Alberta where they had a successful business cattle dealing. They were most hospitable and it was a very enjoyable meeting.

From Calgary we drove down to Great Falls, Montana which is famous for its five waterfalls each of which has a hydro-electric dam and thus it is known in America as 'The Electric City'. So we had covered a fair amount of ground in the first three weeks but the real work now began with our arrival in Rochester, New York State. Incidentally there are no less than nineteen places in the USA called Rochester and four of them are cities. Perhaps the best known even outside America is Rochester, Minnesota, primarily because of its famous Medical Centre – the Mayo Clinic.

My time at Rochester was most enjoyable and productive. The Americans were friendly and accommodating. They had started developing Academic Departments of Family Medicine some years later than in the UK but once started they appeared to move faster. One day they took me to see two doctors who were primarily GPs but they had also trained in cardiology and took referrals in this field from other GPs. My reading of the reason for this was that the GPs' fees for these referrals were considerably lower than those of a hospital cardiologist which poorer patients could not afford. However the GP cardiologists provided an excellent service.

American private medicine at that time was unquestionably amongst the best in the world provided you could afford the fees which were, by some way, the highest in the world. There was, however, an alternative medical service for those patients which the young American doctors said was very much inferior to the latter service in terms of accommodation, staff numbers and quality of service. As a result a number of the GPs in the Rochester Medical School planned to spend some of their early years working among the poor.

They were also very critical of those American specialists who charged very high fees saying: 'Some of these guys spend more time with their stockbrokers than their patients.' Of course all this was back in the seventies and with the arrival of Obama Care standards appear to have risen sharply while Trump's attempt to dismantle the latter failed.

They were all greatly interested to hear about the NHS which gets a poor press in the USA where it is dismissed as 'Socialist medicine'. However the medical staff there acknowledged that the poor in the USA get a service which is grossly inferior to those who can afford private medicine. Neither is it cheap – for example one nurse from a modest background told the story of her mother getting third degree burns, after a fire in the kitchen, requiring grafts. This led to a bill which she had not cleared after 27 years! Even the well-to-do find their bills so hefty so that insurance companies have to employ armies of people whose sole task is ringing patients to urge them to pay their outstanding medical fees.

A Day with Tony

There is also another side to medicine in America and one day I was discussing this with the Professor of Family Medicine at Rochester. I said how impressed I was with his department but, to balance the picture, would he please send me to a GP he would *not* advise me to consult. A smile broke over his face and he said: 'I know just the chap and he is absolutely charming – you will enjoy visiting him. He is an Italian American called Antonio but of course known as Tony." An appointment was fixed at the surgery and we first entered the consulting room which was sparely furnished with a desk and chair for the doctor and a less comfortable looking chair for the patient. History taking was brief, 'Just the main problem' Tony would explain and then a brief examination would follow. He then indicated in most cases the need for a few other blood tests and occasionally X-rays etc. Then we went into a second consulting room where in most cases he left me with the patient as the investigations had not been completed while he returned to take the next history – not a moment was to be wasted. In some cases there were no blood tests etc. and the patients went to consulting room No.2 directly. Tony came along and gave his opinion; prescribed treatment and the patient went to the next room to pay the bill, if it was a simple affair. The patients had a close personal relationship with Tony to whom they were clearly devoted and they addressed him by his Christian name. However it was production line medicine and not in the best tradition of US standards in this field.

Tony took me home for dinner with the family, a wife and several children. His house was enormous and had a huge basement in which the children had cycle races round a track. He had originally been an engineer but he soon realised that he could make a lot more money in medicine. So he retrained in medicine at the age of 27, not because he had a calling to medicine but because he had those children to bring up. I found it rather endearing that he did not pretend otherwise. He worked long hours and made a large salary with the intention of retiring in his middle fifties, but he looked old for his years. Clearly, the pressure was taking its toll and I wondered if his retirement would last for long. I suspect that, if I had raised this point, he would have waived it aside and pointed out that he enjoyed his work despite the long hours and his family and patients were devoted to him.

During my spell at Rochester I came to recognise how well funded and effective US medicine is and, even more so, medical research projects were and no doubt still are. Even the conferences they ran attracted a calibre of speakers well above average. For example one conference, which I attended while I was there, included three speakers who were Nobel Laureates, one of them a famous Englishman, Sir Peter Medawar. He was speaking on 'acquired immune tolerance' which he had discovered along with Sir Frank Macfarlane Burnet (an Australian) and which opened the door to tissue and organ transplantation.

My time at this Medical School was however not without incident. One day I had a telephone call from a young lady doctor called Jane (I forget her surname) asking me to address a local group of doctors on some aspect of the National Health Service. I understood that I would be talking to GPs, as that was my field and I suggested as a subject 'Research in general practice in the UK'. Jane had told me the name of the lecture theatre but I needed directions to get there. She replied that the best thing to do was to go along to the Medical School, which I had been attending daily, where a staff member would meet me and take me to the lecture theatre. This I did and Jane was there to meet me. As she took me along to the theatre she said, 'There's a good turnout and we are all very excited to hear your talk about general practice in England.' This made me distinctly uneasy and things got worse when we passed a large, illuminated sign in the corridor which read, 'A J Tulloch MD, Regius Department of Medicine, Oxford University'. Now I did not have an MD at that point. Then Jane took me into a room to meet no less than four professors who were to be in the audience. My unease gave way to acute apprehension and subsequently, when she introduced me as one of Professor Doll's bright young men, I came very close to panic[3]. However in the end I pulled myself together and stated that I did not hold an appointment in Professor Doll's Department. However I was temporarily attached to the Department pending the opening of a Department of Public Health and General Practice at Oxford University.

By this time I was back on an even keel but I felt that what I had to say was pretty small beer to serve to an audience including such august figures. I also knew that the American medical profession was very intrigued by the British National Health Service which appeared so much more cost effective than their own. I therefore suggested that to apprehend what I had to say in my lecture the audience needed to understand how the British NHS was organised – the Americans always called it 'English' incidentally. They responded with enthusiasm and I immediately started on this tack, inviting them to interrupt me at any point during the lecture if they required clarification. I then spoke for thirty minutes on the manner in which general practice in the UK was organised. Then came a stream of questions and they were particularly intrigued by the fact that NHS patients were referred to Hospital only after assessment by a GP who felt that a specialist opinion was required. The audience acknowledged that the American system, in which the patient went straight to the specialist of their choice, led to them not infrequently to choosing the wrong specialist. This sometimes in turn led to them having to be referred elsewhere which, in some cases, involved duplication of investigations and additional fees for the patient.

While I was involved in this work, the family had been entertaining themselves by exploring Rochester and the surrounding countryside. Several times I joined them, including a visit to the Niagara Falls which, like the Grand Canyon, simply demands attention. These Falls are located on the American and Canadian border and they are made up of three independent parts – the

---

3 Professor Doll had addressed them some time earlier and they had been *very* impressed

Canadian Falls which, as the name suggests, are almost entirely in Canada with a small part is in the USA. The other two are in America and are called the American and the Bridal Veil Falls. The Canadian Falls are in the shape of a horseshoe and they are the largest and most impressive, while the American Falls are rather smaller, though still imposing while the third is much smaller and in line with the American Falls.

In due course, the time came when the family had to return home after six weeks in the USA and Canada. So I arranged for them to fly down with me to New York and we booked into a hotel just off Times Square. At this point my daughter Claire developed Rubella (German Measles) but it was a mild bout and fortunately she recovered quickly. We did manage one day to visit the United Nations Building, which was well worth seeing and we wouldn't have missed the Statue of Liberty for anything. I had feared that the airline would refuse to have Claire on the plane but they didn't. So I waved them goodbye and flew back to Rochester.

Remainder of Trip

Now the time had come for me to complete the trip but I was enjoying myself so much that I stretched my stay in Rochester a couple of days, then I got into my car and drove over to Vermont. It was Autumn, or, to the North Americans, more poetically, 'the Fall' and the trees (especially the maple) and plants were in full bloom. It is almost impossible to do justice to the rich variety of colours created. In addition there had been a moderate snowfall so I had to drive with great care. This was unquestionably one of the highlights of the trip.

I was due to meet Professor Lawrence Weed who held the Chair of Medicine in the University of Vermont, who had devised the Problem Oriented Medical Record (POMR) system which I had used in a modified form for my own project. He had also written a textbook on the subject which I had read before I departed. Now, Professor Weed was clearly a busy man running an academic department, teaching medical students and doing research, so I wondered how much time he could let me have. I remember thinking that if an obscure GP from the middle west of America had arranged to meet a Professor of Medicine in the UK he would have been lucky to get more than half an hour of his time. In the case of Professor Weed it was quite different. He had set aside the morning for me, during which I had two hours of brainwashing on the subject of POMR from him after which I was passed over to one of his Assistants who discussed all the merits and benefits of the system. I was also invited to return next day for the hospital round, which I did. At the end of this I was asked what my impression was of American medicine, having seen a good deal of it during my visit. I replied that in the UK we regard US medicine as up there with the best in the world – if the patient can afford the insurance. If not, the young American doctors have made clear to me that the service to the poorer patients is not in the same class. They appeared surprised that I was so well informed about the twin-track nature of American medicine but I assured them that this was widely known to British doctors. The reader should bear in mind that these views referred to medical care in the seventies whereas today, Obama Care has transformed this picture in the USA despite the determined efforts by President Trump to reverse these reforms.

CHAPTER 11

Care of Patients in Advanced Old Age

a) The nature of the problem

In 1977 I felt the time had come for me to seek an area of general practice in which there seemed to be room for improvement and my attention was directed to the care of people in advanced old age – at that time 70 years or more.

Now when I was a young doctor my favourite interests were in obstetrics (antenatal care and childbirth)* and paediatrics (childcare), while the care of people in advanced old age seemed far less interesting to me at that time. In this group, certain conditions like pneumonia quite often presented in an atypical manner, which made diagnosis more difficult than in younger patients. In addition, response to treatment was more often unpredictable, while neuro-degenerative disorders e.g. severe forms of Parkinson's disease, were much more common in old age and in my early days in practice in the mid-fifties they left GPs feeling quite helpless. Old people in the twilight of their lives at this stage had, on average, just above three medical disorders, requiring treatment e.g. oesophageal reflux (indigestion), but when these conditions are controlled, they quite often enjoy a remarkably good quality of life for their age, providing they remain mobile and can socialise freely. On the other hand cardio-respiratory, neurological and malignant disorders may often seriously impair the patient's quality of life or make them really frail. Last of all are the elite who have managed to avoid serious ill-health throughout their lives.

When I was in practice in Bicester, I came to realise that these old people were far more interesting than I had thought previously. They knew, for example that if they lived into advanced old age many of them would suffer disease, disability and socio-economic problems, which are often more of a problem for older people.

Despite this, it was their quiet resolution so often when I had to give them bad news that impressed me most of all, although they were also very generous. At Christmas I usually received a few bottles of whisky from older patients. It was assumed that, as a Scot, I consumed this spirit but in fact I only rarely had a nip of whisky by this time. Another old lady left instructions that, after she had died, I should be sent a bottle of Drambuie each Xmas for three years and the family duly delivered her bequest. Yet if I am to balance the picture there is also a small minority who can be very demanding, trying and difficult for the carer, if there is one, who may carry a heavy burden. Then I happened to read two research papers on care of people in advanced old age, both published in Scotland.* They drew attention to the under-diagnosis of certain chronic disorders in this age group, partly explained by the tendency of these aged Scots particularly to report illnesses later than they should, just like the English and the Welsh. The conditions most often overlooked in these studies were depression, dementia, disorders of the urinary tract and of the feet, Type 2 diabetes, arthritic disorders, elder abuse and chronic alcoholism. So it seemed that a more active interventionist approach might be required to help these people lead the best life open to them. Last but far from least, is the ageist (i.e. negative) attitude of society in general and carers – familial and professional –towards people in advanced old age.

b) Research Project

I therefore contacted the Department of Health to enquire whether they might be prepared to support a research project in this field. They expressed interest but told me to draft a detailed request for funds to enable them to decide whether they would support the project. This proved more of a job than I had anticipated for I felt that to produce an outline of the project design would take a matter of a few months. However when I asked another more experienced research worker his opinion on the final product he told me that the Department of Health would require more information than I had supplied. For example I had designed a health questionnaire which sought to identify any change in health status and quality of life since the last visit to surgery. This form had to be validated i.e. couched in such terms that it produces accurate and consistent results when used by a variety of different care workers. This again took longer than I expected, with the result that I decided to search for a questionnaire on the paramedical factors likely to affect quality of life which had already been designed and validated. A form designed to meet these requirements had been produced in the Department of Geriatrics at Glasgow University, which was headed by Professor Ferguson Anderson, the first geriatrician to occupy a Chair of Geriatrics anywhere in the world. I wrote to him asking whether he would allow me to use the form now that it was validated. He replied agreeing to this request and he invited me to come up to Glasgow so that he could brief me on the subject personally. Clearly he was intrigued that research in his field was to be done by a general practitioner. I was, of course, delighted and I made my way up to Glasgow promptly, only to find that he had been obliged to deal with some emergency on the day I arrived. It was, of course a great disappointment as I was looking forward to meeting this august figure. However I recall that he apologised profusely and he had asked his First Assistant to take over the task of briefing me. By a remarkable co-incidence he proved to be Dr Francis Caird, who had previously worked in the Oxford area. I had never met him but we had corresponded and he also proved most helpful. He must have spent a couple of hours briefing me on the use of this form.

I then had to draft a detailed description of the design of the project which would take the form of a Randomised Controlled Trial. In this form of assessment, the study population is divided into two well balanced groups using Random Tables to control or avoid bias. These were the Study Group which would be given the new form of more intensive surveillance of patients aged

70 years or more and the Control Group, which continued with conventional demand-led care only, as a means of comparison. So I outlined the plan of the study which required the use of a nurse for some three years at least. The objective was to assess whether a preventive and supportive programme of care using questionnaires and checklists improved health and quality of life for people in advanced old age – 70 years or more in 1977 (today 85 years or more). As an indicator of outcome, I used the time spent in institutional care (hospitals or nursing homes) which, of course, I hoped to reduce to a minimum. I knew this would please both the patient and the Exchequer but I was none too optimistic about the DoH being ready to fund the project. On the other hand, studies of community care in advanced old age were, at that time, pretty thin on the ground. Few GPs then regarded this field as their favourite subject and in this respect I had been as culpable as most of my colleagues during my early years. However my older patients duly took me in hand and taught me that they were the most appreciative and grateful of subjects. In addition I came to recognise that they were also much more interesting than I had previously realised because of the wide diversity of factors involved. These included the socio-economic, environmental, psychological and cultural factors which I described as the paramedical problems affecting health and quality of life in advanced old age. Thus we were trying to find out whether a programme of preventive care in advanced old age improved health and quality of life significantly.

The DoH also appeared to be taking an interest in this subject and in due course they agreed to fund the project. I then appointed an experienced nurse – Valerie Moore – who had worked with me previously and she was to prove an excellent choice. The nature of the problems afflicting people in this age group is complex and embraces both medical and paramedical factors which all need to be taken into account if the patients are to be able to lead the best life open to them. It is hard to believe that general practitioners using a demand-led system alone are as well-informed on the diverse problems of the patients as they should be. Maintaining health and quality of life in this age group is therefore a complex affair. Consequently, we decided to launch the project by thoroughly defining and managing all the medical and paramedical disorders involved.

Health, of course, came first and in the age group 70 years or more these patients will have on average 3-4 chronic disorders requiring medical treatment, but not all serious. This in turn leads to patients, often no longer as sharp mentally as in the past and more forgetful, having to deal with a variety of drugs. At the same time there will be some physical decline and a minority will be distinctly frail, but there is also a minority who, having avoided serious ill-health during their lives, are in remarkably good health for their age. Of course health is an entity which is difficult to define and doctors throughout the world tend to assume that everyone knows what is meant by health, i.e. primarily the absence of disease. However, the World Health Organisation way back in 1948, unhappy with this belief, came up with the definition that 'health was a state of complete mental, physical and social well-being and not just the absence of disease'. This was a first step in the right direction but it could hardly be described as what philosophers call, 'the ultimate nature of reality'. These distinguished figures in the WHO had merely attempted to define health in terms of 'well-being', which they did not define. Thus the waters were as muddy as ever. I would define health as, 'the capacity to adapt to environmental assault (internal and external) and function normally in society' which may be a step in the right direction and would do for the time being. This assault takes the form primarily of medical disorders and their complications plus the side effects of therapy. Alongside these conditions are a variety of other problems which also affect health, quality and duration of life in advanced old age. Some degree of disability and physical decline is virtually universal at this stage and there is a minority who become so disabled that they need institutional care.

Then there are socio-economic, environmental and cultural changes – at this point one's circle of friends, acquaintances and peers is shrinking while the family is less likely to be living locally than in the past and thus they often cannot offer support in a crisis. There is also a minority who have not been able to save much money on their miserable level of pay and are thus reliant on their state pension which alone quite simply is not enough. The result is that they are then forced to turn to food banks where available or simply beg – a public disgrace for the country which is said to be the fifth or sixth richest economy in the world or it was at this point.

Next there are the problems generated by the old people themselves who are often ill-informed about benefits, entitlements and disability aids available for poor, sick, disabled and elderly subjects. Thus they do not always claim these. Lack of regular exercise and obesity may also undermine health as may heavy smoking and drinking. Finally, British people in this age group have been shown to report their illnesses later than other European people in the belief that the symptoms or disorders are simply part of the process of growing old. As I have stated earlier, this can make the prognosis for the patient's illness much poorer and they need careful review and briefing in this connection.

In addition people in this group will be at special risk if they lose a devoted spouse or other close relative, leaving them lonely and isolated. Likewise, at the point of discharge from hospital they may need a good deal of support which is not always readily available and this in turn increases the risk of an early re-admission. Continued health education is vital especially towards the end of life and the main factors which are most important in this connection are company, exercise and purpose in life. The best source of this is either a local History Club which is usually interesting and the University of the Third Age which provides a series of lectures on a variety of subjects as well as interest groups on a variety of subjects. Then there is the need for exercise in the form of walking, for example in a rambling group or taking part in sports activity: Weight reduction if overweight, control of habits damaging to health e.g. excessive eating, smoking and drinking is vital.

Frail elderly people often not being able to afford the home nursing fees is more common than one might think at present – recently it was stated that there are one and a quarter million frail old people in the UK needing institutional care (hospital or nursing home) who could not be admitted for want of beds and lack of money.

In the 1970s my appointment as GP Research Officer at Oxford University came under review since I was originally attached to Dr Acheson's Record Linkage project and when he departed I was left in limbo, unattached to any Oxford University Department. So the University decided that I was to be attached but not appointed to The Regius Department of Medicine under Professor Richard Doll (as he then was) temporarily pending the opening of the Department of Public Health and General Practice. However they forgot to advise the Professor of this change until one day he spotted my name and asked who I was. When he found that he had an obscure GP on his staff in the Regius Department of Medicine, at Oxford University, the outstanding medical school in the UK, it must have been something of a shock but he handled it very well. He came to my room and said that he was intrigued to find that he had a GP on his staff without his being aware of the appointment. I feared that he might be irritated by this matter but he was exceedingly polite and helpful. So I explained that the practice had been working with Dr Donald Acheson on the subject of Record Linkage and he had arranged the appointment originally presuming that it was likely to be a temporary matter. Then when Dr Acheson departed it was decided to make the appointment permanent as the Department of Public Health and General Practice was being developed and in due course I would be transferred there.

Professor Doll then asked me what research I planned to do and I explained that I wanted to screen patients in advanced old age – at that stage 70 years or more[*] – to assess whether screening for medical or paramedical disorders [**]was a worthwhile exercise. I then added that I hoped to do the work by means of a Randomised Controlled Trial (RCT).

At this stage his eyes lit up and he replied, 'You will be the first GP to do this as far as I am aware and I shall arrange for my First Assistant to do an independent assessment when our results are complete.'. Of course, I was aware that Professors Doll and Bradford Hill were the 'fathers' of RCT, which they had used in their famous papers which linked smoking with an increased level of strokes, heart attacks and hypertension. He was pleased to hear of the use of RCTs in general practice.

The project population consisted of some three hundred patients of mine aged 70 years or more, which was regarded as advanced old age in the late nineteen seventies*. This group were divided into a Study Group A and a Control Group B using Random Tables to avoid bias. These patients were sent the Glasgow Questionnaire on the medical disorders from which they had suffered in the past after which they would be sent an appointment at a clinic in the health centre. Then the nurse checked some twenty points which reflected their physical status, after which I did a physical examination and listed, in association with the nurse, all the medical and paramedical problems involved. A programme of care was then designed to address these problems and they were briefed on the best way of dealing with the culture of life in advanced old age.

The first finding was that health was not improved significantly by preventive care assessment in this particular age group. There were minor improvements here and there but these might have improved by chance and therefore were not regarded as significant in the statistical sense of the word. These were hardly surprising findings.

However, in the supportive and educational sense the results were much more positive, as patients felt that a special interest was being taken in them rather than what they saw as comparative indifference to their often complex problems. This, of course, carries a disadvantage for the research worker since if he or she asks the patient whether they feel their health and quality of life are improved they may well exaggerate their response so as not to disappoint the doctor.

Our impression nonetheless was that morale was improved by this programme and this led to the patients spending significantly less time in institutional care (nursing homes or hospitals), which would have pleased patients and the Exchequer alike.

This alone should have interested the DoH, especially as seven other studies between 1979 and 1990 confirmed these findings, but they chose to take no action. In this respect neither were the Colleges of Physicians or General Practitioners the least bit interested despite the fact that reducing the time these patients spent in institutional care would have saved a large sum of money at national level, if all primary care teams were to brief these patients carefully in the interests of optimising their health function and quality of life. This work could be handled by a nurse or nurse practitioner with the GP doing a subsequent physical examination. The problem was that GPs were overworked then and of course they simply do not have the time today. I was, of course, disappointed by the comparative lack of interest in the care of people in advanced old age, which was probably the result of ageism in so many sectors of society at that point, even in professional care workers. In addition the workload of general practitioners since then has risen steadily and they have not had the time to devote to this work. On the other hand I was encouraged by the fact that during the next fifteen years seven studies tended to confirm our findings and subsequent studies have done likewise, with just one exception.

Now, when one has a paper published in one of the professional journals one usually receives phone calls from friends and colleagues in the medical profession to compliment or sometimes to criticise the author on his or her findings. On this occasion I did not receive a single telephone call and neither was I asked to speak on the postgraduate trainee GP programme despite the fact that the GPs who ran this programme were friends and acquaintances of mine. Neither were any GPs in the area doing anything similar so far as I was aware.

However one morning shortly after, I was surprised to hear that there was a call for me from Professor Lawrence Rubenstein in Los Angeles. He said that he had rung to congratulate me for doing the first study he could find anywhere in the world to review the value of preventive clinical care in advanced old age, as well as assessing the best way to keep these patients active and enjoying a good quality of life. He also asked if I would be prepared to go out to Los Angeles and present a paper on the subject, which I did subsequently. I was, of course, flattered by this invitation, especially when I found that he was a highly regarded figure in the field of geriatrics in the USA and he subsequently did research alongside British geriatricians.

Around this time I made the acquaintance of a colleague who had also taken a special interest in care of the elderly. He too had done research in this field and published papers on this subject. His name is David Beales; he is highly qualified and was in practice in Cirencester but is now retired. Together we decided to approach the parties involved in the care of this age group from the Ministry of Health to the Colleges of Physicians and General Practitioners. Dr Beales did this work, only to find the same apathy that we have experienced over the last thirty years. Yet here is a group of people more in need of systemised care than those in advanced old age in which the culture is nearly always radically different? In the case of people in advanced old age today the hope of care along the lines described above is remote. In addition the National Health Service has been underfunded since its inception in 1948 compared with the health services in the other main European Union countries – Germany, France, Holland, Belgium, Sweden and Denmark. France for example, with a population comparable to the UK, spends no less than £20 billion more each year (this figure come from the Financial Times) than we do under the Tory Government at present.

I recently met a former partner of mine and I asked him how things were going in the NHS. He replied **"The National Health Service is in absolute chaos and in some places in meltdown, while GPs are leaving the NHS prematurely.' As a result, the people who suffer most are 'the needy' i.e. the poor, the sick, the disabled, the elderly and old people who are so frail that they require care in a nursing home. They are so frail that they cannot be cared for in the community properly but, all too often, they cannot afford to pay the nursing home fees. So this is yet another example of Tudor Hart's Inverse Care Law which states that the greater the need for a service in society the less likely it is to be available.

Recently the Conservative Party appeared to have seen the light of day, at last, when Mr Hammond, as Chancellor of the Exchequer, threatened to announce in 2019 that in the near future there might be a rise in taxation to cover costs of this sort. In the event he took fright and failed to do this, no doubt due to the risk that middle-class voters would depart the Tory fold if income tax was raised to cover this cost. Now he has been thrown out of the Conservative Party by Boris Johnson, the current Prime Minister.

One old lady put it to me some years ago like this: 'Everyone thinks we are all past our sell-by date.' She was criticising ageism – the tendency of society to view the elderly negatively, especially those in advanced old age. However, even the medical profession is sometimes guilty of ageism, they do not always receive the attention they deserve. As for the politicians, they are the worst of all and every party is guilty. Even when the Blair and Brown governments were in power, there was a need for improvement in this field, but in 2010, when the Conservatives came to power, the economic state of the country became much worse because of their determination to maintain a low level of income tax, which benefited the super-rich, the rich and the well-to-do middle class, often professional people like myself. Mr Cameron, on coming to power, seemed at first sympathetic but ultimately took no significant action in this field. Then he was followed by Mrs May (the daughter of a vicar) and she was so obsessed with Brexit that she completely neglected those in special need, particularly in advanced old age. Finally, Boris Johnston, the current PM, is a right-wing Tory, promising heavier investment in the NHS to meet the needs of patients. However there was no increase of income tax in his plans and without this requirement it is hard to see how he will pay for the improvements he is planning.

I need hardly say that patients over the age of 85 today are the most vulnerable subjects, but do not get a special mention. Later, the PM added £4 billion which was to meet the total state funding of all the government services required, for which this sum was miserably inadequate. The French Health Service for example cost at that time and for a similar population was £20 billion.

c) Care in old age: the need for preparation and careful briefing prior to and during retirement

In this chapter I propose to express the views of Dr Beales and myself on how people approaching old age should prepare themselves, with the assistance of doctors, nurses and social workers as well as volunteers in the future for life in retirement.

In an earlier chapter I described the research done by Moore and I, which established that preventive care programmes in advanced old age – then 70 years or more – had no significant effect in improving health. On the other hand, the effect of such a programme on the paramedical disorders e.g. loneliness, isolation, poverty, loss of a close relative or spouse etc., led to these subjects spending significantly less time in institutional care (nursing home or hospital). These findings were confirmed by seven other studies between 1989 and 1992. Since then more research work has been done in this field, the results of which have – with one exception – been in favour of this approach. Thus one might have thought that, with this body of evidence, that the profession would have made an effort to develop programmes of care, education and support to help the subjects in advanced old age. After all, this was a means of keeping these old people active and independent for longer and able to improve their quality of life. Furthermore, this would have saved the Exchequer a large sum of money at national level.

d) A Textbook on Geriatric Care

Then, some years after my retirement in 1987 along with Dr David Beales, an experienced and talented GP and Michael Denham a respected geriatrician we set out to try and draw the attention of geriatricians and family doctors to the need for a more active and interventionist approach to people in advanced old age. Much of the spadework in this connection was done by Dr Beales, who contacted the geriatricians at the Royal College of Physicians as well as the Royal College of General Practitioners, while I contacted the Ministry of Health. Sadly the response proved entirely negative in each of these bodies.

With the pressure on all the members of the primary care team at present, due to a shortage of both doctors and nurses, there is little hope of this challenge being taken up in the near future. However, Age UK has shown what can be achieved by support programmes. We feel that the programme of care should begin just before patients retire and they should be briefed on the importance of seeking the doctor's advice earlier since a failing of the British is their tendency to do the reverse. By contrast Continental patients consult the doctor much earlier, which often improves the prognosis in serious conditions

As we come to the end of our working lives we look to retirement with keen anticipation as a period of rest, relaxation, exercise, socialisation and freedom from the pressures of everyday work. This ambition is for many middle-aged people quite reasonable but for those with chronic disorders it is rarely that simple. Another problem is that, as the retirement starts, some people are unsettled by the fact that they have so much time on their hands and few tasks requiring to be done. It may take them some time to settle down in their new life. So I would suggest that we need to prepare all these people for retirement by briefing them carefully on the best way to handle this part of their life – from about six months before retirement.

f) The Stages of Retirement

Next, one needs to draw attention to the three stages of retirement and the manner in which they differ:

Early Stage: 65-75 years of age – during this phase most patients are still in good or reasonably good health. However there will be a minority suffering from conditions requiring careful monitoring e.g. diabetes, hypertension or cardiac disorders etc. In addition there will be the paramedical disorders which affect health, function, behaviour and quality of life. Most people in this group enjoy a quality of life which is good, while institutional care and the death rate are both low at this stage. However there will be a small group of people requiring careful monitoring because of medical and/or paramedical problems. Finally the need for institutional care (nursing home or hospital) remains rare in this group while the death rate is also relatively low in early retirement.

Middle Stage: 75 – 85 years of age – the rate of medical and paramedical disorders and disabilities rise in this group as are the rate and duration of institutional admissions but only to a limited extent. The death rate is also rising steadily, especially towards the end of this stage.

Advanced old age: 85 years or more – this is the group with the highest rate of medical and paramedical problems, plus institutional admissions, and the death rate is also a good deal higher. However, it is also the group which is increasing steadily in size in the UK and elsewhere. Thus, especially if you survive into the nineties, your chance of reaching the age of a hundred these days is increasing steadily. Within this section there is a modest group of people who remain in remarkably good health for their age.

This chapter defines the problems of life as we pass through early, middle and advanced old age and our approach should be to develop a programme of care geared to their particular needs in each of the three stages above. This will help to improve their health and function and maintain the body in such a state that disease is prevented or postponed where this is possible. We need also to ensure that these patients are able to lead the best life open to them. This calls for the highest levels of clinical care of disease and disability backed by a periodic screening of their paramedical disorders, especially in the second and third groups.

Later came more bad news that a Covid-19 variant from India called Delta had broken out and it gained ground in the UK steadily. However it has only done this in four or five areas of the UK while the previous vaccinations seem to offer good protection. 'Lockdown' was to be reduced on June 21st 2021, but this may be postponed now.

CHAPTER 12

The Programme of Care for Patients in Retirement

The ideal time for the initial briefing should be some months before the retirement of the patient. The prime objectives are to enable these old people to lead a happy, healthy and socially rewarding life with disease, disability, socio-economic and emotional problems kept under control as far as possible. The friendship and support of a circle of friends is equally important. The first point which needs to be emphasised is that any symptoms which last more than a few days without any sign of improvement must be reported to the General Practitioner as early as possible. British patients must learn the importance of consulting the doctor earlier than in the past when they all too often deferred seeing the GP to much later than their Continental neighbours. We need these patients to be physically and mentally fit as a result of regular active physical exercise while maintaining a diet to control the weight, if this is required. In addition it is very important for these patients to get eight hours sleep each night. Where there is stress the patient should be carefully interviewed and where necessary given the appropriate treatment.

Self-care of the patient is equally important, with the first essentials being good standards of hygiene and exercise. Hygiene in particular must be sustained in settings in which there is a special risk e.g. washing the hands before meals, after using the toilet, after handling animals, gardening, car maintenance etc. Most important of all good hygiene is vital after injury especially, if the skin is breached. The slightest injury of this sort can open the door to infections and thus older people must keep antiseptic readily to hand and use it promptly. This has become even more important now that so many of these organisms are resistant to antibiotics. This programme of self-care is, of course, important in people of all ages but it is most important in the case of people in advanced old age whose natural resistance may be lower than average.

Alongside good standards of hygiene in old people comes the way in which they handle their lives. Exercise for example is just as vital to good health and quality of life as good hygiene whether it is in the form of sports such as tennis, golf or bowls and rambling, which is less vigorous but more long lasting. Sporting types forget that ramblers think nothing of walking seven or eight miles at a time and much more when they are on holiday. Finally, spells in the gym can be equally rewarding.

Obesity is the blight of old age since it is equally the enemy of good health and thus it requires early treatment by diet although vigorous exercise also helps to get this problem under control. The next factor relating to quality of life is in the early stages of old age. Indeed it has been calculated that low levels of social intercourse are twice as damaging as obesity and as harmful as smoking 15 cigarettes per day or suffering from alcoholism. So, forming relationships is very important and if you find this difficult the answer is to join some sort of club and there are a variety of them available in every area in the UK. First there are the sports clubs (tennis, golf, bowls etc) with lots of lively activity, then the rambling clubs with less vigour but scope for the naturalist or bird watcher are equally important. In addition, there is the local branch of the University of the Third Age (U3A) which gives excellent lectures and a variety of subgroups covering photography, foreign languages, table tennis, outings by coach etc. The U3A also run national events in various parts of the country. So it is much easier to form friendships than in the past as a result. History Clubs are also very popular, as are Dining Clubs (generally for males) and Ladies Clubs and Gardening Clubs. Finally U3A clubs mentioned offer the widest range of special interests. To complete the picture, bereavement especially when an old person loses a spouse, partner or other close relative or friend. They often feel they must withdraw from socialising for some days, or more and friends should respect the wishes of the bereaved person while offering help of any sort needed. However patients tend, as a rule thereafter to welcome company and advice whereas others prefer to remain longer alone and their wishes must be respected.

Smoking more than a few cigarettes or heavy intake of alcohol are frequently damaging to health and quality of life and these problems must be controlled or they will contribute to premature patient death. In addition it is vital to ensure that these patients are well-educated in the best ways of keeping fit, and healthy as possible and enjoying the best life open to them.

Then there are the lifestyles of these patients, which vary from the well provided for at one end with reasonably good health, money in the bank, often an excellent quality of life and able to cope even when there is a crisis.

At the other end are the patients who often come from a very poor background, have little or no savings and can barely afford to feed themselves, with the result they have to beg for food at a food bank, a problem which is very rare in other EU countries, but common in the UK. Then there are the usually very old and frail subjects who need care in a nursing home but cannot afford the fees so they have to stay at home, often supported by volunteers, social workers and nurses whose numbers have fallen sharply. No less than one and a quarter million subjects fall into this category in the UK at present – a scandalous state of affairs.

In addition, older people have a new problem these days – criminals who pester those living alone, persuade them that their house needs repair (usually bogus) and they offer to undertake this task. Usually there is nothing to repair but they pretend to have completed the job and they overcharge, sometimes wildly. Other crooks try to persuade these vulnerable subjects to invest money – sometimes large sums – in some bogus project. These old people need to be carefully briefed about these rackets and advised strongly to refuse the offer of any strangers suddenly turning up on their doorstep. So you can see that life in advanced old age can be something of a minefield, especially if the patients are poor, sick, disabled and – worst of all – frail and requiring admission to a nursing home which they cannot afford.

So my point here was that in advanced old age especially there is a need for doctors, nurses, nurse-practitioners and social workers to provide a careful briefing and a regular review, coupled with support when it is required. I therefore suggested that we should meet once a fortnight with the social workers to help provide an integrated service to this group of vulnerable senior citizens. We did this and I found it very successful but two years after I had retired I found that it had been discontinued, which I found disappointing.

Finally the NHS needs instantly a sharp increase in funding and which the then Prime Minister (Boris Johnson) promised some time ago but did not fulfil before leaving office. With the arrival of the new Prime Minister Liz Truss I do not feel confident there will be extra funding for the NHS. The Conservative Party has maintained a low income tax/ low benefits programme from the days of Margaret Thatcher which is designed to keep the well-to-do middle class supporting the Conservative Party.

CHAPTER 13

My Political View of British Premiers since the War

Now at this point I thought it might be interesting to review the activities of post-war governments during my working career and the manner in which they affected my political views, starting with Mr Churchill. I remained interested in the history and politics of the UK and I was and still am, a great admirer of Winston Churchill, without whom I felt we should have lost the war. However I was not eligible to vote in the 1945 election, won by the Labour Party led by Clement Attlee, but my parents, despite their background, were dedicated Conservatives, like so many professional people, and they voted for Churchill. I saw no reason to criticise this action but I began to feel uneasy about the Conservative party later in the post-war years. Britain was then impoverished following the Second World War and the Labour Party did a remarkably good job in the circumstances, especially in introducing the National Health Service in 1948. This removed the fear of the cost of illnesses, accidents etc., which the poor could ill afford. In addition they sought to improve conditions for the needy at a time when funds were low due to the serious cost of five years of war plus our largely unrecognised debts to the USA (the loans given by the USA to the UK during the Second World War). They also nationalised public services and major industries. Thus they could claim in the prevailing circumstances that they had done an excellent job. That certainly was my view and my first ever vote went to the Labour Government in 1951 although I was not a member of the Labour Party.

Then the Conservatives were returned to power in 1951 led by Churchill. To make matters worse, he was beginning to show signs of wear and tear as a result of the terrible strain of the war. It was also suggested by two members of his cabinet that all this was too much for him and that he should give way to Anthony

Eden who made it clear to Churchill that he hoped to succeed him. However Churchill kept deferring his retirement as he lacked confidence in Eden at this point but in 1955 he eventually did retire.

Next Eden took over having won the 1955 General Election. He was tall, strikingly handsome and brave having won the Military Cross in the First World War, in which he lost two brothers. Then, in the Second World War he lost a son. He entered Parliament after this and by 1935 he had risen to Foreign Secretary, an office he held until 1938 when he resigned in protest against Chamberlain's appeasement of the Nazis. Churchill re-appointed him to the Cabinet again from 1940 as Minister of War until the war ended. Then the Conservatives lost the 1945 Election and Eden found himself with the Opposition in Parliament but he remained most popular with the general public. However, he felt that we should maintain close relations with the French to control the Germans but he was opposed to Federalisation in Europe. However his most calamitous venture was to invade the Suez Canal in concert with the French and Israelis secretly. However, support did not come from the Americans under Eisenhower and Eden had to make a humiliating withdrawal. Subsequently he became ill following a botched operation for gallstones in which his bile duct was accidentally damaged and then he developed cancer of the liver from which he died in 1977. I am still voting Labour.

Next came Harold Macmillan whose grandfather was born in the Highlands but his son came down to London to establish a very successful booksellers under the family name. Harold was thus an Anglo-Scot but it is said that he preferred to be regarded as Scottish. Somehow I doubt this as he married the daughter of the Duke of Devonshure, who proved a faithless wife. She had a long running affair with Bob Boothby, a rather shady Conservative MP. Macmillan had been in a succession of important posts during the War and subsequently, including Foreign Secretary and Chancellor. Then he became Prime Minister in 1957 but he resigned in 1963 due to ill-health thus ending a distinguished career. However, despite this he was restored to health and as a result he lived a further twenty-six years. I was tempted to vote Conservative then but I stayed with Labour.

The candidates to succeed Macmillan were R A Butler (Deputy Prime Minister), Reginald Maudling (Chancellor of the Exchequer) and Lord Hailsham (Leader of the House of Lords) with Lord Home a compromise candidate and improbable choice. However Macmillan unwisely threw his weight behind Home and he was appointed PM in 1963. He only lasted a year and he was narrowly defeated in the 1964 Election, after which he retired.

Next came Harold Wilson who had a slim majority in the 1964 Election and he always seemed to me a solid performer who had led his party well. He had also been Assistant to Beveridge in the development of the National Health Service. No doubt because of that I was an admirer although I had stopped voting socialist at about this time and joined the Liberal Party. Then Harold Wilson lost the General Election in 1970 called by Ted Heath.

Heath then came to power and remained there until 1974. It was a difficult time in which he had to deal with the IRA in Ireland, under employment leading to the 'Three Day Week' and miners' strikes. However, he handled these problems quite well. He was a 'One Nation Tory' after the fashion of Disraeli, rejecting the laissez-faire capitalism of Mrs Thatcher who was now his main opponent in the Conservative Party. His spell as PM ended in 1976. Heath was an excellent pianist and a first-class yachtsman but he failed to get the UK into the European Community at first although he was successful later.

In the meantime, Wilson started his second spell as PM. This ended in 1978 and he was followed by Jim Callaghan who had to struggle with a minority Government, industrial strikes and the 'Winter of Discontent, He was a steady pair of hands but this series of events made his government unpopular and he lost the election in 1979. This is the point at which I stopped voting Labour which seemed to me more interested in the welfare of the unions than of the needy and I have remained a Liberal ever since.

Callaghan's loss brought Margaret Thatcher to power and her regime was to last for eleven years, one of the longest of any

British leader. She became very popular within her party and especially with right wing Tories, but she was often indifferent to the plight of the 'needy i.e. the poor, the sick, the disabled, the elderly and the frail. In addition she cut income tax as a gesture to gain the support of Liberals and Conservative alike with the result that she had insufficient funds for the welfare of the vulnerable subjects above. On one occasion, after a speech in which she had rhapsodised about her policies, a reporter asked her 'but what about the poor Mrs Thatcher?' to which she replied: 'Oh they get trickle down' which translates as 'Let them eat cake' in Paris 1790.

Mrs Thatcher said that she wanted to turn Britain into another Singapore and she kept the taxes low with this in mind, at whatever cost to the needy. As a result, she attracted tax dodgers from a number of countries, especially the Russian oligarchs who gave financial support to our football teams and pushed up the value of large houses in London for the ultra-rich. She was an able woman but scarcely brilliant (only Second Class Honours at Oxford) although she proved a shrewd politician with Heseltine the only Tory to take her on. As a young graduate she had applied for a job with ICI and their assessment was, 'headstrong, obstinate and dangerously self-opinionated' – spot on I would have said. As a result we had many hilarious if dubious tales about her behaviour and the best, in my view, told of her going to a restaurant with her male cabinet colleagues. She had just placed her order with the waiter when he replied, 'and vegetables. 'Oh they will order for themselves,' she responded – a good story of course which almost rings true. Finally, the rock on which she perished politically was the 'poll tax'. She welcomed her title of 'The Iron Lady' to which an opponent replied, 'Yes, with a heart of stone.' Mrs Thatcher was from a modest background but she was a hard-line right-wing Tory dedicated primarily to the welfare of the really rich and the affluent middle class. Even they however contributed to her demise. I could never forgive her for refusing to increase income tax to improve the care of the poor, sick, disabled and frail. To put it bluntly, her priorities were wrong.

John Major succeeded The Iron Lady in 1990. He came from a modest background and often this indicates a social climber, but Major never seemed to fall into this category. He was a modest man but the government ran into financial problems in 1992 (Black Wednesday). However, he survived this and went on to consolidate the position of the UK, at the very heart of Europe'. He also paved the way for the Good Friday Agreement signed after he left office in 1997. He set an example for future Conservative Premiers, which they ignored.

Next in 1997 came Tony Blair, the son of a barrister and academic, who had joined the Labour Party – a very rare bird indeed. Good looking and charming he was at first welcomed by the Labour Party. He and his successor Gordon Brown in the early days worked closely together and the latter assumed, since he was the older of the two, that Blair would not stand against him for Leader. When Blair did stand, and won, it ended their friendship. In fact, he was more of a Social Democrat than a Socialist and he alienated the Left Wing of the party by reducing the nationalisation of the economy and the influence of the trade unions. However he remained very popular with the general electorate until, alongside President G W Bush, he went to war in Iraq to drive out Saddam Hussein. This they succeeded in doing but they left Iraq in a state of utter chaos and this damaged his reputation seriously. Finally, after ten years, in 2007 Blair resigned.

He was then succeeded by Gordon Brown, who had a superior intellect to Blair and knowledge of mathematics and economics were his strong points, but he was not the easiest person to work with, lacked charm and could on occasions be explosive. Nonetheless when he ran into a severe recession, he managed to pull the country round before he resigned in 2010.

Thereafter we have had three Tory prime ministers whom I have lumped together since they all have had similar values, policies and objectives but different means of achieving them. Cameron was absurdly young when he was fast tracked into the leadership of the Tory Party and when I expressed surprise by this to a Conservative friend, he said that the Conservative Party was impressed by Blair's earlier success and they decided to select an MP who would 'do a Blair'. At first Cameron, who had never been in a senior Ministerial role before he became PM, gave the impression that he might move to the centre of the Conservative Party by increasing the income tax rate to help generate more money which would finance the public services and in particular The National Health Service. It was a matter of common sense but hard-line right wingers soon squashed this idea. So Cameron conformed to a standard Conservative policy by keeping the income tax rates low in the interest of retaining the votes of many of the Liberals (who had entered into a coalition government with the Conservatives) and thus an overall majority.

As regards his cabinet, he seemed to choose an inexperienced group, largely made up of MPs like George Osborne and Boris Johnson, (who he had been at school with him). None, apart from Cameron, had made any significant impact in the House of Commons, and Osborne proved to be an unqualified disaster. He decided on an austerity programme, not unreasonably, but he extended it much too far. In the NHS, for example, one raft of austerity came after another with staff morale being badly hit. At this point two American Nobel Laureates in Economics – Krugman and Stieglitz – wrote to point out that at a time, when the interest on borrowing was very low, he should borrow as much as he needed and could afford for investment. Osborne ignored them and he was later dropped from the Cabinet as a result, a fate which should have been shared by several other Cabinet members.

Around this time Johnson appeared, with the claim that we should withdraw from the European Union as we would be 'much better off outside on our own'. He gave no explanation whatsoever of why this was the case. However, he had always behaved like a snake oil salesman and he simply gulled anyone who would listen. At this time he was Foreign Secretary, a post in which he appeared to make no impact whatsoever. Finally, Cameron, who opposed Johnson's claim (now called Brexit), decided to call a referendum on the subject, against advice from Ken Clark. However, he was confident that a majority of the nation's voters would support his view but, unfortunately they voted in favour of Brexit. Cameron, wounded and disappointed, ran for the door and resigned.

Next Theresa May was appointed PM and the only major change in the cabinet was that Osborne was dropped. She had been opposed to Brexit but she now decided to support the result of the Referendum wholeheartedly and this she did without much success. Just like Cameron she showed little interest in public services such as health and welfare, police and prison services, teaching, railways etc. They all suffered badly as a result. This uncivilised behaviour started with Thatcher and was maintained in all Tory governments thereafter. In the end she was forced from office by her own party.

Last came Johnson who had first appeared on the political scene earlier as a clownish figure with a silly hairstyle who dropped a brick every so often. It also emerged that he could be a stranger to the truth when it suited him (viz. Max Hastings). Then, he had also been an unfaithful husband in two marriages and was a recurrent 'womaniser' thereafter. However, he has one remarkable ability – the capacity to gull others into believing the improbable or even the impossible. Thus he is Britain's answer to the Snake Oil Salesman from the USA. After all Brexit was never the certainty he claimed and the Tories might surely have found a more appropriate leader for the election since the Governor of the Bank of England expressed apprehension on this subject – he feared that Brexit might destabilise the economy. There were some twenty courageous Tories who expressed reservations about his policies but Johnson quickly responded by expelling them from the party. Once more one might have expected the Tories to regard this response as undemocratic but they remained silent to a man – they too had been gulled, it appears. In the meantime, Johnson sneaked in the back door after manipulating parliamentary procedure and established himself in Number 10 Downing Street. However the Election was still to come and it swept Johnson to victory by a record vote from the Tory Party and due to the unpopularity of Jeremy Corbyn. Since then the Johnson Cabinet, almost devoid of experienced MPs, has been tested by the Covid-19 Epidemic for which they were found unprepared, slow in starting, and wanting in early control. The Germans and the South Koreans were exactly the reverse and their patient death rate, as a result, was far lower than ours. Worse still was the fact that the British death rate from Covid-19 was the second highest in the world to the USA in the early days.

In addition for a deal on leaving the European Union it is already clear that the prospects are very poor and they may well fail to reach an agreement which the Conservatives themselves admit is likely to be a serious matter. Even worse, the National Health Service is under tremendous pressure with ever lengthening waiting list times as a result of chronic underfunding. This in turn is due to the ruthless determination of successive Tory governments to maintain income tax at a very low rate which benefits the rich and depresses the services to the needy i.e. the poor, the sick, the disabled, and most of all the elderly, especially if very frail or living alone at home. In addition, those in the last two categories are often in need of nursing or care homes which they often cannot afford.

I am glad I had the sense to oppose Brexit from the start and now after eighteen months of the Johnson government there is no hint of benefit for the UK whatsoever. It seems as if at the point of our departure from the European Union we may have few gains and considerable losses. After all, the EU has trade agreements with no less than 40 countries at present and is negotiating with a further 30. Just think how long it will take us to catch up on that figure, if we ever do, as a single country. Then there are huge sums due to each EU country from which we will no longer benefit and our poor will suffer from our low income tax rate while the rich benefit even more. Meantime already the more advanced countries in the EU are showing the UK a clean pair of heels as a result of their high rate of income tax. This enables them to fund all their public services, especially their health services, to a much higher level than the UK. France for example, with a population roughly similar to us, was spending twenty billion euros per annum more than the UK eighteen months ago (according to the Financial Times) and Johnson's response was to offer a mere four billion pounds instead. Meanwhile the French will no doubt have raised their figure even further and once again the financial gap between them and us widens.

Finally we are coming to the end of the Covid 19 pandemic by means of a lockdown' in which we all had to stay indoors virtually all the time for 15 months. However, vaccines were, in the end, discovered which got the pandemic under control but only at the cost of 127,000 people dead in the UK. The PM was partly responsible for this figure because he dithered in the early stages of the pandemic but he did better on the advice of the medical scientists when the vaccinations were introduced.

Johnson seems to go from one catastrophe to another. First he had a poor deal from the EU which he has deserved (because of Brexit), then he got into a wrangle with the Irish over the boundary between North and South Ireland. Then lastly the government got involved in a loans scandal in which money was lent secretly from government funds to a firm with which David Cameron (ex PM) was involved. It sounds all very dubious and Johnson who appears not to have been involved has, so far, refused an enquiry which reflects his poor judgement.

Lastly there was a by-election in Shropshire in which Johnson struck rock bottom. It should have forced him into retirement after two and a half disastrous years. However he just went on as if nothing had happened. Furthermore, he was determined to remain PM however calamitous his performance had been. Even worse were the drinks parties he attended for his devotees while he was advising the public of their need to adhere to 'lockdown'.

CHAPTER 14

Towards retirement

When I reached the decision in 1986 to retire from practice in the following year, the first thing I did was to advise my partners of this decision. I had always enjoyed a good relationship with them but now they were looking forward to having a new senior partner with different and presumably better ideas. I had after all been Senior Partner for 19 years and each of my partners had been strongly recommended to us in the first place, which made my task easier, especially as they were almost all 'Oxbridge graduates'. Then we all agreed that the next partner was to be a lady and she too was a very hard working and able girl. However the last new partner was almost certainly the brightest of the bunch since he had every medical qualification open to him except the Diploma in Geriatric Medicine. Yet he wasn't an Oxbridge graduate and the young man was remarkably modest, just like my other partners.

As one's career moves towards its end most of us look forward to leading a different life from the requirements of regular work, although when the time comes some people wonder whether they are making a wise move in retiring abruptly. Would they have been better to go part-time and then retire later they often think? I can only say that I belonged to this group although I was very happy working in general practice which is a rewarding but also demanding job. In the Oxfordshire practice we worked from 8.30am till 6.15 pm each day except Thursday – my half day which I gave up when I took up the Oxford appointment. In addition, we were on call for emergencies in the evening and night one day a week as well as one weekend in five. My partners did likewise and most other practices followed this pattern. Now when the GP is in his twenties, thirties or even forties the burden is quite easy to carry but by the time he or she has reached the fifties and sixties it is another matter. For this reason, I had no doubts of my need for retirement, although I worked three mornings a week for the practice after retirement visiting the elderly in a nursing home over some five years. I also maintained for two years my appointment as a GP Research Officer.

I was 61 years of age when I retired and I was in good health and physical condition although I have mild aortic stenosis (a leaking heart valve) first diagnosed about 10 years before I retired. Now I am still going strong although my exercise tolerance is in decline, but I can still walk two miles on a level road, at the age of 96, without tiring. All this surprises both my cardiologist and myself. However I was forced to give up tennis when I was 86 due to a torn ligament in my right shoulder, but this does not hinder my golf as the left shoulder does the work in this game – for the right hander. I think, looking back, that I have squeezed into my life a good deal of different forms of activity, experiences and interests. Mind you they did not all come off – for example I did not take up skiing until I was in my early thirties and the result was that I reached average standard only. My problem was that at five feet six inches I was much too short for tennis although in squash and badminton it seemed to matter less, provided you were fast about the court which was never a problem with me. Finally in my nineties I have become more forgetful.

Christine and I were both keen on foreign travel and we have visited most of the major countries in the world except India.

Politics has also been an interest over the last seventy years and I have almost always voted Liberal although I admired Churchill (in the wartime years), Macmillan and Heath among Tories and Attlee, Blair and Brown from the Socialist Party. The Liberal Party leaders varied a good deal but with one exception they were respectable performers. I could not stand Mrs Thatcher with her inadequate trickle down for the poor. Of the last three Prime ministers Cameron and Mrs May were well intentioned but the sooner the Conservatives draw the curtain on Johnson the better. Max Hastings, a distinguished historian and Johnson's boss as Editor of the Daily Telegraph in the past, once described him as utterly unsuitable for this type of post. That is good enough for me. He will never raise income tax to the level needed to fund all our public services, especially the NHS, properly and who will suffer as a result? The poor, the sick, the disabled and the frail requiring nursing home care, which is in short supply currently and things are getting steadily worse. When I was in practice the NHS was constantly underfunded irrespective of which party was in power. The British like to do things on the cheap, I fear. However in the last ten years things have become steadily worse as reflected by the constantly lengthening waiting time for operations and the widening gap in standards when compared with the EU countries. Then along came Johnson sneaking in the back door to Number 10, determined to maintain a low income tax policy which left the public services even more *highly* underfunded. At the same time he gulled the Electorate into believing that Brexit would make this country much more prosperous. In reality our departure from the EU has been a disaster to date and I am sure there is more to come. The advanced countries in the EU are simply leaving us well behind – Germany, France, Holland, Belgium, Sweden and Denmark, with Germany a clear leader. None of these countries has an English style Conservative party although Germany & France each have ultra right wing Conservative parties which are kept under strict control. The reason for the success of these EU nations is in high income tax rates which can fund public services generously. Meantime the Tories are intent on keeping their income tax rates low in the interests of keeping the middle class voting for the Conservative Party, at considerable cost to the country. My case rests your worship.

 Clearly since I am now 95 my days are numbered especially as I now have to cope with nominal aphasia. Doctors love sententious words and phrases and I plead guilty myself. It means that I am becoming more forgetful and it is socially embarrassing when I cannot recall the surname of an old friend I haven't seen for several years. However I hope to hang on a bit longer. I cannot complain whatever happens as fate has been very kind to me.

Retirement is for most people a well-earned relief with the keen gardener having time for his horticultural recreation while the sportsman does likewise on the tennis courts or golf course etc. Then there is the would-be traveller who starts on European holidays, but this needs a well-stocked bank account. Also there is the public-spirited group who give up part of their week to visit old people in need. Others in retirement do not always find it easy to pass the time of day as they have no interest in any of the above topics and as a result find retirement more disappointing than they had expected, although they usually adapt to this situation in the fullness of time.

As regards my own retirement I fear that I am not much of a gardener although I mowed the lawn, did a bit of edging and hedge clipping until some six years ago when we acquired an excellent gardener – to my great delight. Paul is the hardest working person I have ever known. The requirements in retirement are purpose and contentment in life at this stage alongside activity and companionship. I have been spared major problems and at my age I am still in remarkably good condition physically. However, I am well aware that at this stage the 'Old Reaper' might call at any time.

My wife and I had also acquired a taste for foreign holidays, with skiing in the winter for me but less often my wife who had never been keen on the sport. Then we departed to various parts of the world in summer such as Hong Kong, China, Singapore, Australia and New Zealand.

In retirement as we grew older our holidays tended to be mainly in Europe, the Mediterranean, North America and Argentina as our younger son had married a delightful girl from Buenos Aires.

I forecast, by the way that South America will become much more popular in the future, especially Argentina, Brazil, Chile, Peru plus Costa Rica in Central America. However, both Argentina and Brazil are politically and economically unstable at present, which may be discouraging tourists from visiting these countries. Yet they, along with Chile, have rich natural resources and breath – taking scenery. On the other hand Costa Rica is politically stable, has no army and is regarded as the arbiter of disputes and peacemaker of Central America, which has been badly needed in the past. This was a trip we enjoyed especially.

When we changed to more river cruising in Europe with my wife who comes from an Anglo-Russian family, we chose St Petersburg as the first port of call. Christine's family had gone there in the 1840s but they still regarded themselves as English three or four generations later! As a result when the Revolution came in 1918 they were regarded as suspect by the Communists. All this despite the fact that her father had taken Russian nationality earlier while retaining his English nationality. They had 48 hours' notice to leave Russia in 1919 and one branch of the family went to Finland where they settled for the rest of their lives. Christine's father, on the other hand, came to live with relatives in Birmingham and made the city his home for the rest of his life. St Petersburg proved an excellent choice for us as it is a handsome city with lots of beautiful architecture as well as symbols of the Czarist and Communist eras. For example, we boarded the ship which fired the gun that started the Communist Revolution itself, best known as, 'Ten Days that Shook the World' This was the title of the most famous book which presented the Communist Revolution in 1918 and gave the most accurate picture at the time of a rebellion in which the brutal Czarist regime was replaced by the equally brutal Communist version.

We also sailed down the River Volga, which we found less picturesque than other European rivers, although we were impressed by the huge locks ordered by Stalin himself much earlier, most of them embellished by equally large statues. Moscow proved also to be a striking city with its very large and imposing Red Square surrounded by highly distinctive buildings, some of them painted in bright colours, quite unlike the august buildings in St Petersburg, some of the latter castles. While in Red Square we also entered a building in which the body of Lenin lies embalmed, a miracle of preservation when you remember that he died in the mid-1920. However, the body looked unnatural and the atmosphere in the darkened room was eerie, with the result that we did not linger there very long.

Thereafter we sailed on most of the rivers of Europe which enabled us to visit cities like Amsterdam, Berlin, Vienna, Budapest, Salamanca, Paris, Lyons, Helsinki, Oslo, Rome and a number of others. We enjoyed them all but our favourite was the Rhine with German castles on the banks, some still occupied but most in ruins. In addition, the colourful old buildings were equally impressive and colourful dating from the 14th and 15th centuries in some cases.

There were also trips in the Mediterranean visiting a variety of interesting cities.

CHAPTER 15

The Evolution of Western Medicine

Discoveries and Advances

This has been my main hobby in the last decade of retirement so far and I wish I had started it earlier when things were fresh in my mind. However I thought that readers might be interested if I made a brief journey – acting like a timeline – through this subject with special emphasis on some of the great discoveries in the field of Western Medicine. However it behoves me first to point out that the earliest efforts at healing were undertaken in China, India, Egypt and Mesopotamia. We know this from the relics of the skulls found all over the world with signs of trepanning to relieve suffering dating as far back as circa10,000 BC.

Western Medicine however started much later, around circa 500BC and it began the Humoral Era which lasted to the end of the 18th Century. Its unscientific belief was in Humors, a system of medicine detailing the make-up and workings of the human body. It was mainly associated with Hippocrates on the island of Kos. He was the first to believe that illness was caused naturally rather than by superstitions or the influence of the gods. In addition he listed a series of recommendations for good and successful care, of which the best known was *primum non nocere* – 'above all do no harm'. They were called the Hippocratic Oaths. He was aided by several other famous philosopher scientists of whom the best known were Archimedes and Aristotle. This was Greek medicine and it was the most dominant of the era. Then Hippocrates came to be known as the 'Father of Medicine' and he also started the Hippocratic School of Medicine. The other famous doctor at this stage was Galen, a Greek whose approach was to remain until the end of the 18th century, using the Humoral Method of care. The Greek Era lasted from circa 500 to 156 BC.

```
              YELLOW BILE
                  /\
             HOT /  \ DRY
                /    \
   BLOOD      <        >      BLACK BILE
                \    /
             WET \  / COLD
                  \/
               PHLEGM
```

The Humoral System

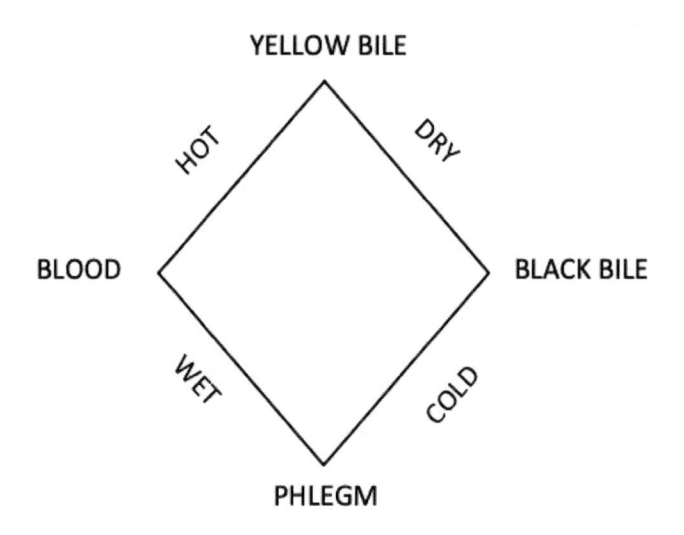

The Humoral System of Medicine consisted of four Humors – yellow bile, black bile, phlegm and blood. Then these were linked to what was regarded as the four basic elements of the world – fire, air, earth and water. Each of the humors would wax and wane but they were in balance when the subject was healthy. Imbalance meant ill-health, thought to be caused by vapours inhaled and absorbed by the body. Each humor was linked to a season, and they were also associated with an element and an organ; they were also associated with 'qualities' (rather like symptoms today), names and characteristics.

Finally the Hippocratic Oath was taken by all medical students until relatively recent times.

Next came the Roman Period from 156 BC to the third century AD in which Galen moved to Rome and remained the most influential figure in medicine there although there were several other important Greek doctors there. They were the first to identify the classic features of inflammation – heat, redness, swelling and pain and they were the first to classify disorders according to their location – conditions of the skin, ears, nose, teeth and sexually transmitted diseases, which had previously been neglected. However, apart from philosophy, the Romans were a more cultured and sophisticated race than the Greeks. They built teaching centres, buildings for the sick, roads, drains, sewers and aqueducts.

Galen remained the most influential figure of the Roman Era. He was strongly influenced by the teaching of Hippocrates and thus he used the Humoral System. Nevertheless, he was the first to develop the experimental method in medicine based on the study of anatomy and physiology (using pigs) and he was also the first to discover that arteries carried blood. However he failed to realise that the heart acted as a pump and was a twin track affair which required a communication between two ventricles and these he claimed to have found. In fact no such ducts existed.

The other important figure of this era was Avicenna, a Persian, who too was regarded in his era as the 'father of medicine' and famous for his five-volume work, 'Canon of Medicine', which became the standard work on this subject internationally.

16th Century Advances

In 1543 Andreas Vesalius, a major Flemish figure and a keen researcher, published an important volume, 'On the Fabric of the Human Body' which revealed faults in the teaching of Galen.

Next came Ambroise Pare a French barber surgeon who made his name on the battlefield by changing the older method of cauterising wounds with boiling elder oil and replacing it with a topical ointment, which proved much more effective. He also reintroduced ligatures to control bleeding (Galen had originally recommended this). He too was seen as the 'father of medicine' for his era.

17th Century

William Harvey (1578-1657) An Englishman who after a period of meticulous research discovered that the heart was the pump which helped to circulate blood from the right side (atrium to ventricle) and thence via blood vessels to the lungs for oxygenation. From the lung the blood leaves via the left side of the heart (atrium to ventricle) and again by arteries to the capillaries. Thence to the capillaries and veins which, by this time, take venous blood back to the right-hand side of the heart (atrium to ventricle). This completes the circulation.

It was a remarkable discovery, but one which was not widely accepted at first in England or on the Continent, especially since it contradicted Galen. However, later doctors on both sides of the Channel came round gradually to a recognition that Harvey was correct and Galen's views on circulation were discarded. Harvey was also the first to suggest that human beings reproduced by means of a male sperm fertilising a female egg. As result he received many awards – Physician to Kings James I and Charles I, Fellow of the Royal College of Physicians, Oxford University, and others.

Thomas Sydenham (1624-89)This Englishman was regarded as the outstanding clinician of his age and he came to be known as 'the English Hippocrates'. He is also thought to be the first doctor to attempt to classify disease by systems. His most famous dictum was, 'Go to the bedside, there alone can you learn disease.'

Richard Wiseman (1622-93)Another Englishman, he was Sydenham's counterpart in the field of surgery, mainly on the battlefield in which he set high standards which led him to be known as 'the Father of Surgery' in England at least.

18th Century

This was of course what philosophers call, 'the Age of Enlightenment'.

At the University of Leyden, which had displaced the University of Padua as the outstanding medical school in the world, worked Hermann Boerhaave (1669-1738), a Dutchman who was emerging as a major figure and a great admirer of Sydenham. He was a great intellectual, an impressive lecturer and a first-class clinical teacher. In addition, he produced the best textbook written up to this point by drawing on a wide knowledge of medical and scientific subjects.

James Lind (1716-94) was a Scottish naval doctor who is credited with discovering that fruit juice prevents scurvy, which he reported in 1753. In fact it was first reported by a Portuguese sea captain, Vasco de Gama, in 1498, but the latter was not a doctor and did not publish a paper on the subject. As a result his claim was not taken seriously and the use of fruit juice was given up by the navy for a considerable period. So it was a rediscovery, although Lind was not aware of de Gama's claim and thus he gets the credit because he published his own research findings. Of course, he did not know why the fruit juice worked as vitamins had not been discovered in 1753[4].

William Hunter (1718-83) and John Hunter (1728-93) were Scottish brothers who came down to London as trained surgeons with a deep interest in anatomical research and teaching. William's research was primarily on bone and cartilage while obstetrics was his chosen specialty. Both developed successful anatomy schools and both became Fellows of the Royal Society. William became Court Physician to Queen Charlotte while John became Surgeon General to the British Army and he made a number of

---

4 By this time in the fields of science and medicine, a discoverer was only recognised as such when he or she was able to explain the nature of the discovery.

discoveries in medicine and surgery. Between them they laid the foundations of modern surgery.

Edward Jenner (1749-1823) was an English doctor who in 1797 was to make an important discovery when he noted that the milkmaids having contracted cowpox did not subsequently develop smallpox. He therefore vaccinated some sixteen subjects who all had been treated with cowpox and confirmed their immunity to smallpox. His most famous case concerned the son of his gardener, James Phipps, an eight-year-old in whom the vaccination was also successful. The clergy opposed vaccination which they called 'repulsive and ungodly' but Jenner held the line and overcame the opposition, unsurprisingly as smallpox could be very disfiguring. Mind you, this process had been introduced to England earlier in 1721 by Lady Mary Wortley Montague, the wife of the English Ambassador to Turkey, after she had noticed its use. However she was not a doctor and had done no research work in this connection.

William Smellie (1697-1763) was another Scot who did his training in Glasgow after which he went to Paris and London for further instruction in obstetrics. He was the first doctor to study childbirth scientifically and to describe the mechanism of labour. He had an obstetrics practice in London and he became a much sought-after teacher. He is now regarded as the 'father of obstetrics'.

The 18th Century also saw the opening of many hospitals

19th Century

This era saw the dawn of scientific medicine with improvements in the understanding of the nature of disease and its management. Advances came more widely than previously and there was a variety of important discoveries. Three countries were responsible for the majority of these discoveries. The Germans and the British made the most discoveries with the French right on their tails, with the most important single discovery of the century – organisms. Also Rene Laennec developed the stethoscope and Paris became the most impressive medical school in the world.

Germans who made major discoveries:

Van Helmholz (1821-94) invented the ophthalmoscope, which greatly improved the diagnosis in eye disorders and he was also involved in the study of sensory and nerve physiology.

Johannes Müller (1801-58) who did important research which greatly improved our understanding of the nature of sight, speech, hearing and voice. Also, he made important discoveries about fermentation and digestion but his main achievement concerned propagation of the importance of cells in all tissues.

Rudolf Virchow (1821-1902) shared Müller's views on cell theory. However when asked to investigate an epidemic of typhus in Upper Silesia he blamed the outbreak on poverty, poor education and deprivation. He also emphasised the importance of the microscope in understanding diseases. Furthermore, he is regarded as the father of modern pathology

Robert Koch (1843-1910) had the most formidable record of all since his research identified the organisms responsible for anthrax, cholera and tubercular disorders (TB) for which he was awarded the Nobel Prize. However his attempts to provide a vaccine for cholera were only partly successful.

Wilhelm Röntgen (1845-1923) announced his discovery of X Rays in 1895 – one of the greatest discoveries in the history of medicine, for which he was awarded the Nobel Prize.

Paul Ehrlich (1854-1915) advanced the theory already produced by Elie Metchnikoff that the defence system was based on the formation of antibodies. Both of them were awarded the Nobel Prize

O Minkowski & J von Mehring demonstrated that by removing the pancreas of a dog they produced diabetes.

British doctors who made important discoveries:

John Snow (1813-1858) After four serious outbreaks of cholera in England between 1832 and 1866 with heavy loss of life, Snow, an Englishman, transformed the situation by establishing that the infection was waterborne and removing the handle of the Broad Street pump. This reduced the frequency and severity of cholera attacks. Thereafter better standards of hygiene further improved the situation. He achieved this by checking the mortality rate in the vicinity of several pumps which made him 'the Father of Epidemiology'. He was also an early pioneer in the use of anaesthetics, especially in childbirth and he used chloroform during some of Queen Victoria's deliveries.

Joseph Lister (1827-1912) An Englishman who was an outstanding surgeon. He worked for most of his career in Edinburgh and Glasgow but his place in medical history is down to his pioneering use of antiseptics to prevent or control any infection and often this saved the patient's life. His work was first published in 1867. His dressings were soaked in carbolic acid, which controlled the infections far better than in the past, and later he sterilised his instruments. He was the first to admit that his programme of antiseptics was based on the work of Louis Pasteur and indeed each greatly admired the other.

Sir Charles Scott Sherrington (1857–1952) FRS and PRSA. A brilliant Englishman, at Cambridge he started as a surgeon and took his FRCS as well as the FRCP. Then he moved towards research in physiology. His areas of interest were pathology, histology, bacteriology and neurology with the latter being his prime interest. He named several parts of the brain such as "synapse" and the term 'proprioceptive'. He later won the Nobel Prize in association with Professor Adrian Hill.

Lawson Tait (1845-1899) was a Scot, worked in Birmingham as a surgeon and who took Lister's antiseptic programme even further when he introduced asepsis, which can be described as the state of being free from pathogenic micro-organisms (bacteria, viruses, fungi and parasites). This is achieved by adding to the Lister method of antiseptic dressings and better standards of hygiene by more intensive measures – even higher standards of hygiene, better operating clothing and better methods of sterilising instruments etc. He also did pioneering surgery on the gall bladder and in gynaecology.

Ronald Ross (1857-1932) an Anglo-Scot who discovered in 1897 the life cycle of the parasite (plasmodium vivax) in malaria responsible for the transmission in the bowel of one genus of mosquito – the anopheles – for which he won the Nobel Prize.

Other fields in which the British made major advances were in hospital organisation, improved personal hygiene and nursing especially by Florence Nightingale. This also pioneered public health and epidemiology.

Hungarian who made an important discovery

Ignaz P Semmelweis (1818-1865) a Hungarian obstetrician who anticipated Lord Lister and Lawson Tait in reducing the rate of infection after childbirth. He compared the rate of puerperal sepsis in pregnancies handled by medical students and by midwives. The rate was significantly higher in medical students than nurses. He attributed this to the fact that nurses rarely attended post mortems and surgical operations. He therefore recommended higher standards of hygiene prior to childbirth and on operation. However some of his colleagues were unconvinced and many of them refused to accept his views. Only later was his place in medical history confirmed.

The French also made important discoveries

Rene Laennec (1781-1826) was trained to listen to chest sounds by placing his ear on the chest directly or when he listened using a quire of papers rolled into a tube and heard chest and heart sounds more clearly. Then he designed a tube made of wood and brass which was even more effective and it came into general use in France and elsewhere. The modern binaural stethoscope was invented by an Irish doctor, Arthur Leared, in1851, and it is now in general use as the preferred choice.

Louis Pasteur (1822-1895) was the outstanding figure of the 19th century both for his discovery of micro-organisms and their importance as a cause of infection. Germ theory had dated from the Middle Ages but he was the first to confirm the belief scientifically. He also developed the understanding of vaccination, fermentation and pasteurization. As a result he reduced mortality from puerperal fever and in addition created the first vaccines for rabies and anthrax. Finally, he strongly recommended better hygiene to prevent infections, yet he was not even a doctor but a highly trained biologist and chemist – a very remarkable man indeed.

Marie Curie (1867-1934) was born in Warsaw but went to France to study under Pierre Curie and Henri Becquerel and all three won the Nobel Prize for Physics in 1903 for their work on radioactivity. She was the first woman to win this prize and in 1911 she won a second Nobel Prize, the first person to do so in a second field – chemistry. Like Pasteur she too was a very remarkable scientist.

The French had also developed an outstanding Medical School at the Salpetriere Hospital in Paris, staffed by an excellent set of teachers and clinicians. They were particularly interested in neurology and psychiatry. Edinburgh was the only other medical school to come close to matching them at this stage until the early nineteen thirties. The Edinburgh Medical School in particular pioneered ante natal care clinics and was second to the Paris School in the Victorian age.

20ᵗʰ Century Discoveries & Advances

Karl Landsteiner (1868-1943) a German immunologist classified blood categories as A, B, AB & C and drew attention to incompatibility and rejection. As a result, in 1907 came the first successful blood transfusion. In addition along with Popper and Levaditi he discovered the polio virus in 1909. He was also awarded the Nobel Prize in 1930.

F Gowland Hopkins (1861-1947) an Englishman discovered vitamins in 1912 which are vital to health, growth and survival. He was awarded the Nobel Prize along with C Eijkman in 1929

Paul Ehrlich (1854-1914), a German, discovered Salvarsan in 1908, an arsenical and the first drug effective against syphilis which came to be known as 'the magic bullet'. He was awarded the Nobel Prize in 1908.

Paul Dudley White (1886-1973) an American who developed and pioneered the use of the electro-cardiogram, which greatly advanced the investigation of cardiac disorders from the fifties. He was regarded as a superb teacher and a compassionate bedside clinician.

Edward Mellanby (1884-1955) was a major figure in English research who discovered vitamin D and its role in rickets, then very common in the slums of big cities in Britain. He was a formidable figure who was elected Fellow of the Royal Society in 1925. He also acted as secretary to the Medical Research Council from 1933-49. Finally he was knighted (KCB) in 1937 and GBE in 1948.

Discovery of Insulin

F Banting (1891–1941), C Best (1899-1978) & Prof. J J R Macleod Prof. B Collip

This discovery was perhaps the most remarkable of them all. The man who set the ball rolling was Fred Banting who was neither a brilliant scientist nor had he any previous experience of research work. He was trained as a GP surgeon and had just started in practice when he had this 'great idea' of tying off the pancreatic duct of a dog and then studying the effects on the pancreas and the blood sugar. Professor MaclLeod, Chair of Physiology, University of Toronto, with a special interest in carbohydrate metabolism, set up Banting and provided him with one of his two most brilliant students, Charles Best and Clark Noble[5] to undertake the biochemistry involved as agreed in the above project. In addition, he raised the money required and provided accommodation and equipment needed. He also had to brief them on how the research programme should be conducted. The project began in May 1921 with Banting operating and Best undertaking the biochemistry research. Dogs were to be used for the research and it soon became clear that working conditions were well short of ideal. The working room on the roof was covered by tar melting in a hot summer. The room had to accommodate an operating table with equipment plus a bench for biochemical work. There was also a stench from dead and dying dogs. To begin with progress was slow and during this period it generated stress between Banting and Best. In addition, Macleod was away for two to three months visiting European research centres with an interest in diabetes after a holiday on Skye. Then Banting and Best began to improve their technique, especially with Dog 92 which survived four days in good health after the pancreas was removed – much longer than other dogs before, and with that their morale was raised further. Macleod returned in early August and was pleased to find that there were clear signs of progress although some of the work had to be repeated. Now he was much more optimistic than at the outset and

---

5 It soon became obvious that in the cramped workroom in which they worked there was insufficient space for both Best and Noble to work together. Thus on the spin of a coin Best won, but the deal was that they would alternate every few months which proved impossible and so poor Noble lost his place in medical history on the spin of a coin.

he promised to do everything in his power to help. For a start he advised that they use Ringer's Solution to preserve tissues. They had now devised a pancreatic extract which they named "Isletin", later changed to "Insulin" by Macleod. Thereafter it was steady progress up to late November when Banting and Best gave the first presentation on this subject under the title 'The Internal Secretion of the Pancreas' which went off very well. However, Banting stumbled at question time and Macleod had to get him off the hook which Banting resented! Progress thereafter was steady until December by which time they had established that their extract was effective in animals but not in human beings. At this point Professor Collip, an able biochemist from Calgary University, offered to purify the Banting and Best extract, which he did over a period of six weeks. Then the insulin was tested and found to control the blood sugar in animals and human beings alike with Leonard Thompson, a fifteen-year-old boy, being the first diabetic to be treated successfully with insulin on January 23rd, 1922.

Thereafter in the next two to three years the developmental and exploratory work had to be done to explain the nature of the discovery. Meanwhile Banting and Best had advised the Canadian press that they were the discoverers which, after all, was only a half truth. Meantime Banting had developed a corrosive hatred of Macleod whom he suspected of trying to steal his discovery and Collip had (for a time) come to regard himself as the discoverer of insulin – another half-truth. However, when the Nobel Prize was awarded in 1923 the awards went to Banting and Macleod only. This followed the Nobel Committee's view that their Prize should go to only one or two of the people nominated in most cases. One of these is nearly always the Professor heading the department and the other is the prime discoverer in the department. However Banting was furious that Macleod was included at the expense of Best and he announced that he would share his prize money with Best. Macleod instantly responded in kind by sharing his prize money with Collip. Best was also furious and it is easy to understand why.

Discovery of Penicillin

Part 1: 1928.
Alexander Fleming (1881–1955) – a Scot – physician and microbiologist

Part 2: 1940.
Howard Florey (1898–1968) – an Australian biochemist
Ernst Chain (1906–1979) – German refugee, biochemist
Norman Heatley (1911–2004) – English Biochemist

This was a biphasic piece of research with Fleming discovering Penicillin accidentally in 1928 and writing a paper on the subject which was accepted and published. However, after a further six years along with five other practices, all of whom failed to explain the biochemical nature of the discovery they gave up in 1934. The reason for this was that none of the teams included a biochemist. Then, six years later, Professor Howard Florey with two outstanding biochemists Chain and Heatley completed the biochemical assessment at Oxford University within three months and they announced this important discovery to the world in 1943. In addition, they struck a deal with an American Pharmaceutical company to produce large quantities of Penicillin for wounded servicemen particularly.

Ernst Ruska (1906–1988) a German who announced in 1932 that he had designed an electron microscope which had 400 power magnification now increased to two million power magnification. This was a very important advance in microscopy as doctors could now see the previously invisible viruses.

Gerhardt Domagk (1895–964) another German who in 1936 announced his discovery of sulphonamides, which proved very effective in chemotherapy, especially against staphylococcus and streptococcus but it could produce marked side effects in some cases.

Robert Shatz and Selman Waksman – these two Americans announced in 1943 that they had discovered streptomycin, which is a cure for tuberculosis and thus a tremendous breakthrough. However it did not take long for resistant strains to emerge. Nonetheless this effect was offset by combining the drugs para-aminosalicylic acid (PAS) and isoniazid.

Important qualifying factor – see end of this section[6]

Percy L Julian (1899–1975) was an American who, in his early career, suffered as a result of anti-colour bias. Nonetheless, he proved to be a very able research chemist and pioneer in the chemical synthesis of medicinal drugs from plants. His work laid the foundation for the industrial production of cortisone and other corticosteroids useful in asthma, rheumatoid arthritis, autoimmune disease and some forms of cancer. He was also in the team which discovered progesterone and testosterone.

Jonas Salk (1914-95) an American virologist and medical researcher who in 1955 announced an inactivated vaccine, given by injection, against polio, a very disabling disorder. It appeared to be effective and was widely used. However there are a number of strains of the virus and the first intestinal strain was not always affected.

---

6 Important qualifying factor in the discovery of streptomycin. The nomination for the Nobel Prize went to Professor Selman Waksman only, which excluded Albert Shatz, the team member who actually made the discovery. The Nobel Prize Committee made their decision, unaware at first of Shatz's primary contribution, due to the devious and deceitful behaviour of Waksman. At this point Shatz wrote to the Nobel Committee and pointed out that he was the prime discoverer, but they refused to add his name to the Prize. The irony of this was that Waksman could have had his name on the Prize in any case alongside Shatz but he wanted all the glory to himself and the Nobel Committee supplied it. For more details read 'Experiment Eleven', 2012 by Peter Pringle.

Albert Sabin (1906-93) an American researcher, announced in 1961 an oral attenuated vaccine which proved more effective against the intestinal strain than the Salk vaccine which it displaced.

Howard Schaeffer (1929-2017) and team. American-led, they revealed in the seventies the discovery of acyclovir which was effective against herpes zoster and against chicken pox in the immuno-compromised.

Gertrude B Elion (1918-1999) An American lady chemist who shared the Nobel Prize with George H Hitchings and Sir James Black for their innovative methods of drug design in the development of new drugs. She worked for an English company in New York (GSK). In the eighties came the anti-retroviral drugs which prolonged lives quite a long time in AIDS sufferers without effecting a cure.

In 2004 came the Mapping of the Human Genome which started in 1984 and is now completed. This is expected to be very valuable in a variety of fields. It helps us to understand diseases better and to identify the true nature of viruses. Thus treatment can be improved and it is likely to be particularly important in oncology. The 20th century has also provided a greatly improved understanding of the immune system of human beings and the way in which it works.

CHAPTER 16

Looking back

As I look back down these many years now, I feel that I have had a variety of interests and elements of good fortune. My parents were a blessing for a start and my sister and I got along well after a poor start. So, there were no stresses in the family. I had a good school record having taken six Higher Qualifications for University entry but when I went to Aberdeen University the competition was raised and I became a face in the crowd. Still, I enjoyed my school and university years.

Then, during my two years in the RAF I spent eighteen months abroad in the Middle East i.e. Canal Zone, Egypt and the Sudan and I enjoyed every minute of it. No, not quite – I had bacillary dysentery once and I wouldn't impose that on my worst enemy. However, when I went into practice I approached the job differently from most other doctors. I spent two years in hospital posts in preparation for general practice which very few budding GPs did in those days – the fifties – but I was single and could afford it. I had of course overlooked the need for a wife and when I did get a job as a GP it was offered because I was single!

No wife would put up with her husband being on call 24 hours a day, seven days per week, unless he asked to be off duty. The senior partner made some additional concessions after two years at the weekends but I was still on duty through all the nights for seven years – I was able to go out but when I came back to my flat above the surgery I was back on call.

It seemed to me that alongside ordinary clinical care I wanted to look for areas in which there was a need for improvement. My choice was record keeping, and care of the elderly came into this category, and from that point on things seemed to fall into my lap. I was offered an academic post at my old medical school but I was settled and happy in England and I turned it down. Then

I was advised to contact a senior academic at Oxford University named Donald Acheson, who was especially interested in record linkage along with two colleagues. I was offered the appointment but the senior partner in the practice announced that he had decided to take up the offer himself. It was a disappointment for me at this point but it was to be a much greater regret for the other two parties. Later, I was offered the post in my ex-partner's place at Oxford University and this time I accepted the offer. I published a series of papers in the next 20 years and this made my career even more interesting and enjoyable.

I was even fortunate in my partners in both practices (Coventry and Bicester alike) and it was especially generous of them to allow me, in the Bicester practice, to take up the offer of GP Research Officer at Oxford University one day per week, including my half day. It was the lowest form of academic life but I enjoyed the work and few practices had a better record system than ours after I undertook an MD thesis on the subject. Later I decided to extend the system to my partners in addition and they welcomed it. For this I needed a nurse trained in this work and the Department of Health seemed ready to fund the system when they read my thesis. Later they offered to maintain and update the system. They hoped that other doctors, having seen the system, would improve the standards considerably. Sadly only some twenty-five doctors did so, although some of them wrote a book on records to which I contributed a chapter.

Then there was the occasion when I told Professor Richard Doll that I wanted to do a Randomised Controlled Trial to evaluate a Preventive Care Programme in the Elderly. His response was encouraging, especially as he added that if I achieved this I would be the first GP to do so. I have always regarded the RCT as a method of research originally designed and introduced by Doll and Bradford Hill in their famous work on smoking and lung cancer.

Nurse and I went ahead with the study and published the paper on care of the elderly. However it provoked little interest in the UK despite the fact that its findings were confirmed by six other studies subsequently – five British and one Dutch. Care of the elderly was hardly ever a special interest for GPs. However, I was invited later to give a talk in Los Angeles on the subject, which I accepted. Valerie Moore, the Research Nurse and I were even more pleased when our paper was quoted six years later in the best geriatric textbook available for GPs in my entire career – 'Practical Geriatric Medicine' by Exton-Smith and Weksler. It was an excellent Anglo-American publication but I do not know how well it sold.

My disappointment was that the record system I designed for my MD thesis has only provoked interest among 20-30 GPs, so far as I was aware. Yet a computer man told me that if it had been introduced nationally it would have made computerisation by technicians far easier, quicker and as a result also much less expensive. Now when you think that there were some thirty thousand GPs at that time. If each had a set of A4 record files using the Problem Oriented Record System and then add the figure for hospital doctors, which would almost certainly have more than doubled this sum, and you can see that the waste of money ran into millions. That was the view of a computer expert I met at a conference some years later. I learned one important lesson from him in my professional life. I found the Ministry of Health always very generous when one sought money for research, however modest the subject, especially if one had a university appointment. However, I wonder whether the results are subject to appraisal at the Ministry of Health, since I never had any comments on any of my papers.

As regards my other interest in care of the elderly, I am sure that clinical care today is vastly better than when I first went into practice in 1954. However, I believe that most people approaching old age would benefit even more from a careful briefing on the subject of life in retirement and especially in advanced old age. The British have a weakness for reporting their symptoms to the doctor much later than other patients, in the European Union, for example, and this has got to stop. Lastly we need to identify and manage the factors other than disease which mediate good health and quality of life. Age UK is already showing us the way.

Finally, what of the future? Well, the Conservative Party is in power for at least another four years and with a hard-line right-wing Tory PM. However, Johnson's pathetic performances at the Despatch Box is coupled with an undercurrent of resentment in the House of Commons as it begins to be recognised that Brexit is proving a myth already. Even some Conservatives have said that if we do not get a good deal on leaving the European Union it would be a serious matter. I support the Liberal Democrat Party but its previous leader, Clegg, who had seemed so promising, mishandled the deal with Cameron and it cost him his seat in Parliament. What we need is a strong centrist independent Social Democrat Party which has served the Germans so well and they have three variations of social democratic branches. Incidentally I have just been reading 'Why the Germans Do it Better' by John Kampfner and I strongly recommend it. No wonder that they are the most influential country in the EU, especially with Angela Merkel at the wheel. Could you imagine any of the present UK Government matching her? The PM's determination to keep the low income tax policy can only lead to our public services becoming even more impoverished and the rich getting richer while the poor get poorer. The result is that we have 14 percent of our population 'living in poverty' at present while 1 percent of the population hold 50 percent of its wealth and a significant number of them have squirreled at least part of their money in foreign havens for 'legal' tax avoidance. Poor Cameron was embarrassed when he found that his father was among them. The low tax policy is designed to keep 'Liberal' Tories and Middle-Class voters on board and it is very effective if the 2019 Election is anything to go by. It astonishes me to hear NHS doctors bitterly critical of the present government who then vote for the Tories – I wonder why.

On the other side of the English Channel and the North Sea there are six countries – Germany, France, Holland, Belgium, Denmark and Sweden – which drive the European Union. Their governments, led mainly by Social Democrats, have high income tax rates which allow them to fund their public services generously. Their health services are also particularly well endowed and they are steadily leaving the UK behind in this field. The French for example spend £20 billion more on their health service than we do in Britain with a roughly similar population. The British response from Johnson two years later was a mere four billion pounds and he will never raise the income tax to close that gap because it keeps his party in power. He neglects the 'needy' i.e. the poor, the sick, the disabled and the elderly in making the rich richer at the expense of the poor. There are no Conservative parties as we know them in the EU countries although there are Ultra Conservatives in France and Germany which they are keeping well under control. Low income tax in the UK remains the problem and one man is primarily responsible for this policy – the present occupant of No.10 Downing St. However, Keir Starmer, the new Labour party leader, is already showing signs of taking him to the cleaners when they meet at the Despatch Box. Surely the time has come after ten years of Tory rule with three indifferent Prime Ministers.

Cameron was the first PM of this ten years and from the outset it was obvious that he lacked the experience so vital for a Prime Minister and on appointment he had not even held a single ministerial office. However, he was handsome, well intentioned and charming even giving the impression that he might increase taxation although he never did. I pointed this out to a Conservative friend who replied, with a smile, that the Conservative Party had been very impressed by the early years of Tony Blair. In the end Cameron developed into the standard right-wing Tory and when his Brexit Referendum went wrong he made for the door.

Next came Theresa May, the daughter of a Vicar who had been a 'remainer' over the Referendum. I thought she might increase income tax to meet the requirements of the poor but I was wrong. Then she charged around the world trying to arrange trade deals before the Conservative right wingers forced her out.

Finally came Boris Johnson who slipped into Number Ten by a back door. His personal history was simply appalling – membership of the odious Bullingdon Club (like Cameron), betrayed two wives (unlike Cameron) and then became a serial womaniser. We were also given a scathing report by a former editor of The Daily Telegraph, who had been his boss, and who described him as a stranger to the truth, a colleague who regularly appeared for meetings poorly briefed and wholly unsuitable to be Prime Minister.

Nonetheless, he was elected to power with a huge majority. Alas, we have to put up with another four years of Tory rule in which the gap between the rich and poor in the UK is by a Factor of 127 compared with 100 for Germany which is a much better run and wealthier country than Britain. The result is that they, along with several other European countries, are leaving the UK behind.

The Prime Minister knows that higher tax is absolutely essential if public services are to be properly funded. This problem began with Cameron who appointed Andrew Lansley as Ministry of Health, an old family friend. He set out on a programme to privatise the NHS which proved to be expensive and disastrous. Since then, the cost of the NHS has risen steadily and waiting times have gone up pro rata.

The waiting times for operations have also risen and there is a great shortage of nurses and doctors. Now, instead of training more doctors they have imported doctors and nurses from abroad where they are sometimes badly needed. Then we hear frequently of the rising length of waiting lists and of the shortage of funds. The result has been that our NHS is way behind countries like France and Germany and this will remain until the UK electorate drops the Tories. I feel that this means our waiting till the next election but there are signs that I may be wrong. As a result of the recent Amersham and Chesham result I feel we may get there earlier. I wonder whether the 'blue wall' is beginning to crumble. After all. It would be sensible for reasonable Tories to recognise that leaving the EU was a major bloomer and Brexit makes it even worse because of the poor deal with the EU which followed plus another bad deal over the Irish border. Likewise his dithering over the opinion of the Medical Scientists aggravated the already enormous death rate in the UK pandemic – the fourth worst in the world. Next time he acted very promptly on the advice of the Scientists with much better results. Even the dreadful Johnson can't get everything wrong.

CHAPTER 17

The Scots Nationalists

Now this book was supposed to end here but I cannot end without commenting on the Scots in politics over the last 14-15 years, especially as I am a Scot who has worked in England where I have lived happily for sixty-nine years. Previously I had lived equally happily in Scotland at the educational stage when there was great rivalry with the English on the sports field especially at Wembley and Twickenham. Alas, the English are far too strong.

Both nations were opposed to nationalism after the First World War and the English have maintained this attitude ever since. The Scots however were taken over by the current Scottish Nationalists some 16 years ago and the political view they held was that they were more capable than their three UK neighbours and would be far more successful if they went independent. Now the Scots have a remarkable reputation for discoveries and new developments in the past but they seem to have been less productive recently.

As so often in a field like politics, the Scots are again hardly highfliers in invention these days and this is just the point where Nationalists move in, flatter their victims and offer to run the country led by a prominent Nationalist. The first Leader was Mr Salmon, a glib if sometimes amusing speaker, accompanied by his much younger sidekick Nicola Sturgeon. She is good at presenting a project but she was clearly not to be trusted, as when she promised that if the government granted the first Referendum on independence it was to be her last such request. Promises are meant to be kept Nicola, but I have lost count of the number of times you have broken your promises in this connection alone. However, more recent polls show that the Scots are getting less enthusiastic about nationalism at the moment after a recent election.

At that time Nationalist Scotland was run largely as a duopoly (husband and wife) but now it is a one-girl band. For example, if there is a new project in the Scots Health Service the Minister responsible never presents it to the British public, as Sturgeon always presents everything. She takes over and leaves the Scots in no doubt that she will remain for a prolonged period – rather like Putin. Yet what are the benefits she has brought about during her reign? Two years ago, the standards in education fell and the shortage of funds for the Health Service is just as bad as in England. In addition, she has alienated the European Union by trying to break up the UK and she has been warned that she should not assume that Scotland under the Nationalists will be accepted by the EU. Finally, she debars all Scots living in the UK outside Scotland from voting on such an important issue because she fears most would vote against independence. The source of this problem is Anglophobia but I rarely find any serious criticism of the Scots in England. The English are much more tolerant. There was always a small minority of Scots who were Anglophobic when I lived there and the present nest of Scot Nats have gone out of their way to cultivate them.

Finally have all these Nationalist Scots ever estimated the cost of going independent? It would be a repudiation of the other three countries who are among your best customers at present, but not if the Nationalists succeed. The Scottish Tourist Board will be furious as their numbers start to fall due to alienation of their best customers.

The Scots mineral resources have gone, along with their shipbuilding and they are reliant on fishing (already in decline) and farming. Even recently, Glasgow businesses were expressing fears about the adverse effects on them of independence. Finally, just think of the cost of having to erect accommodation on every road into England plus the cost of staff. If you are hostile to your neighbours it becomes a costly game, and there is much more besides. Yet more than half of the Scots support independence under the Nationalists and I know of no other civilised country which has been a success under any Nationalist government. Still the PM may insist that expatriate Scots must still have a vote if they live in the UK or he may simply refuse the demand of the Nationalists or both. I cannot see the Scots prevailing in this foolish exercise and Nationalism is a stupid game wherever it emerges. The PM will never allow it and for once I am on his side, as I do not want to see Britain carved up at the will of the Scottish Nationalists.

Finally : One parting thought for doctors. Medicine, at the end of the day, is just what you make of it – coupled with a bit of good fortune. I was no more than a face in the crowd as a student but I have widened the base of my interests in medicine and I have not given up even now. I wish I could say the same about the British Medical Association, which appears not to have protested vigorously enough about the gross underfunding of the NHS. As a result, this very day (15th April 2021) it has been announced that 4.7 million operations are being delayed more than a year, which is a public disgrace. It is caused by the low tax and low benefits financial programme operated by the Conservative party which makes the rich richer, the middle class (including me) more affluent and neglects the rest. Fourteen percent of the population are 'living in poverty'. Food Banks are proliferating for those who cannot afford to buy what they need to survive. Also around a million people who are too frail to be in the community cannot be admitted for nursing room care because of a shortage of beds. The Prime Minister of the present Government is most unlikely to amend his policy and my fear is that the British are going to be shown a clean pair of heels by the European Union. The last time the French health service was raised by 20 billion pounds more than our NHS the PM responded with 4 billion pounds. My case rests your Worship

My only regret is that I am now 95 and I am almost certainly not going to be around when the next election is held even though I am currently quite fit for my age. I am, however, more forgetful and at times this is rather embarrassing. So I do not want to hang on for too long.

Thus this tale has come to an end. I hope you enjoyed it.

CHAPTER 18

Covid–19: A Viral Pandemic

Finally came the Covid 19 virus infection in some four or five waves with the dreadful loss of over 127,000 lives in the UK during the first year. It began in Wuhan China and spread round the world. Because of a dithering approach by the PM and his cabinet the UK suffered the fourth highest death rate in the world. Also the management was of 'lockdown in the homes'* except when people were obliged to go out on essential shopping and business only. Everyone was also obliged to wear masks in these two locations and also in shops, etc. All familial visits were suspended

The duration was around eighteen months and it seemed to be recovering with the aid of vaccinations when we had a second wave of 'variants' which were less severe. Then came a third from India called Delta which has now established itself in a number of centres in the UK.

However a number of vaccines were discovered of which two were produced in Oxford – Pfizer and AstraZeneca – and they were among the majority chosen for the job.

Also the response to a double injection has been very successful with a small minority having side effects. This has been great news for us all but at the same time we must bear in mind those sad families which have had to bear the loss of a much-loved family member.

It has also been a miserably wet autumn and winter (2021) but things are now looking up and the British morale seems to be rising or at any rate it was until I read this morning's paper. The public have tired of waiting for an end of 'lockdown'. They feel that by the end of July they should be able to get back to normal life. The Government is more Conservative since they fear that they might be hit by a fourth or fifth infection. Of course they are right and for once I agree with them. We have to remember that Covid-19 came from Sars a few years earlier. The public, however, are not pleased now that we have those new vaccines and today's paper reports public restlessness and crowds protesting in the street. I doubt that we shall get complete freedom from 'lockdown' until mid-Summer and the main complaints come from the Education Service and those who have booked a holiday abroad, which includes the Tulloch family. Still, once again I support the Government. We must always bear in mind the grievous losses in the first wave of Covid 19. It took two years for this to settle down but the lockdown and vaccination gradually had the condition under control in the UK.

CHAPTER 19

Past thoughts

I must express first of all my gratitude to my wife who has been most helpful in the writing of this book. Christine is a bright girl with a remarkable memory which turns me green with envy. She is a trained Medical Social Worker and her main recreation is reading novels. Now, with the family having long left home she has time for her hobbies – gardening and rambling. Her endless patience and support throughout my career has also been a prime benefit to me.

Without our wives particularly it could have been so much more difficult for any GP to cope with the burden. Perhaps a tale will illustrate my point. At the height of winter with snow on the ground one evening I went to bed early as I was on call, only to be wakened just after midnight.

A call came in from a patient with chest pain and it sounded like a heart attack. So the patient had to be seen immediately. My home was six miles east of our surgery and the patient was in a village six miles to the west. So it was a return trip of twenty-four miles with snow falling and an icy road. The patient did have a heart attack and so I had to remain with him until the ambulance arrived half an hour later. I then drove home slowly over icy roads to find my wife awake and very worried. She was concerned in case I had had an accident and another call had come in from a patient in the same village I had just left. This time it was a woman and she too had to be seen. So I went to see her; she had acute abdominal pain and this time the ambulance arrived promptly, shortly after me. She departed immediately and so did I, but my wife was in tears when I returned a second time and it was easy to understand why. I am glad to say that I never had in the rest of my career any call which even approached this combination of hazards. However General Practice can be very stressful for the wives.

I am also grateful to the family who have all been most helpful in the production of the book itself. My daughter Claire went to school at Headington School in Oxford. On leaving school she went to study for a degree in Social Policy and Administration. She then secured a place on the NHS Management training scheme in Nottingham working in a range of roles until she left the NHS in 1997 looking for a change of direction. After a year out travelling in Australia, New Zealand and Asia she returned and changed careers in 1999 to become a conference producer. She subsequently worked in a number of different companies including Emap, UBM and Ascential where she became a Conference Director. She met her now husband Ian in 2014 and relocated from London to live in Northampton. She married in 2016 and is now living very happily in a village outside the town, Great Houghton. She left her last permanent role in 2017 and is now a freelance conference director and also runs an agency, TEMBO Content.

My eldest son is Graeme, who we opted to educate privately in Oxford firstly at the well know Dragon prep school, followed by secondary school in St. Edwards just off the Woodstock Road. After successfully completing his A' levels he then moved on to complete a Geography M.A. at Edinburgh, which teed him nicely to start his career in the drinks industry, working for Guinness Plc, which subsequently became Diageo. Graeme based himself in Chiswick in London where he met and married Amelia in 2001. In 2005 Graeme left Diageo and moved on to become a Commercial Director at Dunnhumby Ltd, which took him travelling to a number of exotic locations and an expat assignment in Cape Town, where he based his family for 6 years, between 2013-19. Following this exciting adventure to South Africa, Graeme returned to London, where he now works in partnership with his brother Ross running their own business specialising in Franchising. Graeme & Amelia now live in Chiswick where they have 3 delightful daughters – Daisy, Lilla & Tilly, who are growing up fast!

My youngest son is Ross. Like his elder brother he was educated at the Dragon and St. Edward's school in Oxford, before going on to study European Studies at Cardiff University, where he captained the Men's Rowing team and won a blue. After university, he joined British Airways' graduate scheme and spent a number of years with them, including a stint living in Argentina, where he met his future wife Agustina, before moving back to London and subsequently out to Reading with his two children, Nico (a keen footballer) and Isabella (who loves art). He subsequently worked in various Sales director roles for Expedia and Groupon, covering both the UK and Europe, before going into business with Graeme to run a chain of Subway franchise restaurants. Ross and Agustina also have an Irish Terrier, Sandy, who comes to stay with Christine and I when they go on holiday.

Perhaps my greatest achievement was to survive the arrival of three Oxbridge graduates into the practice! Only joking – they were all excellent clinicians and good friends so that there was never any dissension between us. I also owe a debt of gratitude to my partners for allowing me a half day away from the practice for years to take up the post of GP Research Officer at Oxford University. So I worked on what had been my half day and I enjoyed every minute of it while my partners covered my patients who needed care on the day. The cash generated on my half day was, of course, paid to the practice to reward the other partners.

Alistair and Christine with their children Claire and Graeme in 1969

Tulloch Family in 2021, Alistair and Christine with Ross, Isa, Ami, Daisy, Tilly, Nico, Lilla, Agus, Ian, Claire & Graeme

Alistair and Christine with their grandchildren, Isa, Daisy, Nico, Lilla and Tilly in 2021

CHAPTER 20

What of the Future?

Well at 95 one has to accept that my life prospects are limited but I remain reasonably fit physically and I am still playing golf two or three times per week. I walk with my wife several days each week some three kilometres and I was also still enjoying life until the virus disorder Covid 19 came along in February 2020 and made life much less enjoyable. I only go into Bicester now about once each week from Wendlebury. My wife is very protective and keeps me on a lead most of the time. I have had some thoughts about preparing people for life in old age before they retire and I may turn out a paper on this subject before I go.

The other problem is Brexit – short for British exit from the European Union. This was the work of Boris Johnson who managed to gull his own party and a significant minority of the Labour Party into believing that we would be far better off by leaving the European Union. He made no attempt to explain why this was the case.

The Electorate, including a significant minority of Labour supporters, accepted his claim at the subsequent Election. Indeed they went even further and returned him to power with a huge majority. So the die was cast and Johnson was convinced that he could negotiate a suitable deal with the European Union. In the ultimate event the negotiation went on for months and the PM managed a deal which was a pale shadow of his original ambition. Of course the EU had never wanted the UK to leave their organisation as they had anticipated that the British electorate would vote against such a move.

The EU were, of course, operating a high tax/high benefits programme which enabled them to finance all their public services and care for 'the needy'. By contrast the UK was exactly the reverse with 14 percent of the British economy 'living in poverty'.

Also the number of beggars in our streets rose sharply and many have had to sleep in the open. In addition, numerous adults and children were saved from starvation by food banks supplied by noble donors and volunteers. It was clear that if Britain had stayed in the EU they would almost certainly have come under pressure to adopt a similar programme. Johnson was not having this and having won the election he assured the electorate that his programme, which came to be called Brexit (from British Exit) was the answer and the British would be much better off using it.

Around this time Johnson decided, under pressure from staff in the National Health Service, that he must make substantial funds available for this Service and he supplied four billion pounds. Now this was a substantial sum but far short of what was needed as indicated by the comparable French figure mentioned earlier. The result is that a good percentage of the population are begging for food supplied by food banks. There are also increased numbers of people sleeping in the open. Finally, many frail old people cannot be looked after properly in the community because they cannot be found a place in a nursing or care home. This is a public disgrace for the United Kingdom, run by the Conservative Party, which refuses to raise funds to care for the 'needy' and sick.

Waiting times are also getting longer while GPs and nurses are in short supply. The taxes should have gone up long ago. Just imagine the bewilderment of the advanced EU countries – Germany, France, Holland, Belgium, Denmark and Sweden – with their generous levels of taxation, finding that the British have to get by on far lower levels in the UK. This, of course means that the wealthy benefit as do the moderately affluent (to which I belong) while the unemployed and the poor are impoverished further.

I am vicariously ashamed that the government of a once great nation of whom I was proud to be a member is now operating a low taxation policy. This yields utterly inadequate funds which cannot meet the needs of public services. Perhaps the best example currently is the devastation of the National Health Service as a result of underfunding over a long time. Consequently patients requiring an operation may find that surgery is deferred for twelve months and in some cases for a further year thereafter. I need hardly comment on this state of affairs.

In addition successive governments have failed to increase the number of trainee doctors required to meet the increasing burden of work in the NHS. Instead they have offered work to people in countries abroad in which the need for them is even greater than in the UK – a disgraceful policy.

Likewise recently doctors and nurses have been required to cope with a much heavier burden for which their payment was increased by just one percent.

Then along came a new Chancellor of the Chequer called Sunak, clearly more Liberal in his views compared with the past of the PM and his Cabinet. His policies were soon paired down and he looked rather sheepish as he presented his policy. No comment is necessary.

Finally I understand that there is a movement within the Tory Party which wants to increase privatisation of parts of the NHS. Are they keen to move nearer to the American policy model I wonder?

Now, one asks, why do they operate a low taxation policy when a rise would solve their problems? The answer is simple as it is designed to keep the Tories in power at any price.

I cannot end without a suggestion for the Opposition parties in which everyone is terribly polite and lacking in aggression – not exactly ideal for a bruiser like our PM.

From the start of the Covid-19 virus infection the medical scientists reporting daily gave us excellent clear cut graphic presentations of the progress of the pandemic. This approach can be used in the field of politics as well and it can be very effective. First of all you should form a group of Opposition party leaders who would employ a team of two statisticians and economists to monitor political progress in a form which is clearly understood by the general public. In health, for example, a comparison of the NHS performance with that of Germany, France, Sweden, Denmark, Belgium and Holland would be very revealing. I forecast that the UK would be way behind the EU countries.

The rather diffident leaders of the Labour, Liberal and other parties should bear this in mind. They need to hire an economist and a statistician to compare the UK figures for expenditure with the above countries and the hopeless inadequacy of the Johnson Government would soon be clearly exposed.

CHAPTER 21

Final chapter

Now I have reached the last milestone of this book of mine. Six years ago it was discovered that I had aortic stenos caused by an abnormal heart valve. The condition was very mild and the cardiologists suggested that there was no need for any action at this point. Thereafter I have been seen annually and to the astonishment of the specialists there has been very little change until last year and the change at this point still remained very modest. Thus surgery was still not required to my relief but the likelihood was forecast that in February 2023 I may require to have operative intervention subject to my own approval. This will be a difficult decision for me and my wife but we shall take the decision only when the cardiologist has expressed his view.

Of course when one reaches the advanced age of 96 the old reaper cannot be too far away but my day-to-day health has remained remarkably good thus far. My only problem has been recurrent bouts of sneezing marked by a loud barking sound well above the average for a man of five feet six inches only.

The crunch will come in March when the cardiologist will have to use two machines to assess the decline in cardiac function. Then he will assess the degree of failure. If the decline is beyond a certain point the cardiologist will assess whether a risk of operating at this point will be too hazardous and thus he may advise against surgical intervention. The family in this situation are usually more likely to oppose surgical intervention at this point because of the risk in a man of my age.

My own opinion is that my health remains remarkably good for a man of my age – 97 years of age next May. I still play golf three times a week and I frequently go for a walk of two miles with my wife. So the cardiologist is unlikely to recommend surgery at this stage. However congestive heart failure can be a dangerous disorder so we must hope for the best.

In addition with Cov19 back on the scene again this year my doctor has arranged for three vaccinations in the past and I am to have a fourth today by coincidence. So I shall hope that fortune smiles on me again.

So I shall end with a favourite quotation:

> "The Moving Finger writes, and, having writ,
> Moves on; nor all your Piety nor Wit
> Shall lure it back to cancel half a Line,
> Nor all your Tears wash out a Word of it".

The Rubaiyat of Omar Khayyam

I hope also that you have enjoyed the book.

Finally I must express my grateful thanks to those members of my family who have been most helpful: Christine, Claire, Graeme and Ross.

Most helpful of all was a neighbour called Pat who was an expert on computers and this proved most helpful.

Summary of my career

A.J.Tulloch MD FRCGP
1950 Mb ChB Aberdeen University.
1950–52 Medical Officer RAF – UK & Middle East.
1952–63 General practitioner Coventry.
1954 Foundation Member Roy.Coll.Gen. Practitioners (RCGP).
1963–87 GP Bicester, Oxon.
1969–89 GP Research Officer, Unit of Health Care Epidemiology, Oxford University (one day per week).
1970 Invited to join the Committee of the Thames Valley Faculty, RCGP (TVF).
1972 Nuffield Travelling Research Fellowship for three months USA – American record systems.
1973 Upjohn Travelling Research Fellowship UK for one week: Integrated Patient Care, UK.
1973–74 Chairman Thames Valley Faculty RCGP.
1976 MD Aberdeen University: Medical Records.
1976 Elected Fellow RCGP.
1976–77 Provost TVF RCGP where I met the Duke of Edinburgh.
1986 The Medical Annual- Subject 'Preventive care of the elderly in the community' by A J Tulloch & V Moore.
1987 Retired from practice but carried on the research for two years.
1991–2001 General practice member on the Medical Research Council Study of preventive care in the elderly.
Other subjects are described in the book.
When one enters the field of medicine one little thinks of the many paths one may tread and the destinations one may reach. I was, after all, merely a family doctor without *special* talents. However there were newer paths to be taken if standards were to be raised

Alistair J Tulloch 31.10.22

The author

Born and raised in Scotland, AJ Tulloch trained as a doctor at Aberdeen University before undertaking his two-year National Service in the RAF. Having qualified as a GP in 1950 he worked in Coventry for two years before becoming a partner in a practice in Bicester. He developed special interests in Structured Records Systems, something that could have saved the NHS millions and care of the elderly.

In 1987, at the age of 61, he retired and since then has travelled widely, accompanied by his wife Christine. These adventures have taken them all over the world, including many river cruises in Europe. He was a keen sportsman, though at the age of 95 he finds a brisk walk suffices.

In Medicine and Other Topics he also offers forthright opinions on the state of the NHS, politics, and fond memories of colleagues in Britain and America.

Alistair Tulloch has three grown-up children and several grandchildren and lives in Bicester, Oxfordshire.

novum PUBLISHER FOR NEW AUTHORS

The publisher

> *He who stops getting better stops being good.*

This is the motto of novum publishing, and our focus is on finding new manuscripts, publishing them and offering long-term support to the authors.
Our publishing house was founded in 1997, and since then it has become THE expert for new authors and has won numerous awards.

Our editorial team will peruse each manuscript within a few weeks free of charge and without obligation.

You will find more information about novum publishing and our books on the internet:

www.novum-publishing.co.uk

Printed in Great Britain
by Amazon